YOU CAN
BE YOUR
BEST

Starting
TODAY

Books by John Mason

You Can Do It—Even If Others Say You Can't

Believe You Can—The Power of a Positive Attitude

Be Yourself—Discover the Life You Were Meant to Live

YOU CAN BE YOUR BEST

Starting

TODAY

JOHN MASON

SPIRE

© 2012 by John Mason

Published by Revell
a division of Baker Publishing Group
P.O. Box 6287, Grand Rapids, MI 49516-6287
www.revellbooks.com

Spire edition published 2015

ISBN 978-0-8007-2340-8

Previously published under the title *Let Go of Whatever Holds You Back*

Printed in the United States of America

15 16 17 18 19 20 21   7 6 5 4 3 2

To Dave, for his joy that reminds me
to have a smile on my face.

To Mike, for his energy and inquisitiveness
that remind me to be creative.

To Greg, for his patience that reminds
me to take small steps.

To Michelle, for her love of music that
reminds me to live a life of praise.

To my wife, Linda, for her commitment to God
that reminds me to be a man of right priorities.

To Mom and Dad: Dad, thanks for being a great
example of the right kind of father and husband.
I miss you. Mom, thanks for loving your only
son and for always being there for me.

Contents

Contents

Part 2 Looking Outward

═ Part 3 Looking Upward ═

Acknowledgments

Heartfelt thanks to some great friends:

Mike Loomis, for your humor and agreement

Tim Redmond, for your sincere insight into my life

David Blunt, my dear pastor friend, for whom
I have the highest admiration and respect

Introduction

Momentum—a great word for a powerful life. I believe without a doubt that God's will for you is momentum. He wants you to let go of whatever holds you back. His best is for you and me to grow, increase, and be more than what we are today.

I'm a big sports fan. I love basketball, football, golf, and many other sports. (Yes, I even love *watching* golf.) Of course, the word *momentum* is frequently mentioned in nearly every event I watch. Why? Because it's such a key to a team's or individual's success. Those little successes building one upon another lead to the best results. I recently heard a basketball coach on the radio saying, "We've got momentum. We've won nine games in a row. We expect to win every game we play now. The players are more confident when they shoot and consequently make more shots."

Here's why I wrote this book: I want you to win more games and make more shots. As you read this book, I believe you will capture and increase momentum in your life. The Bible says you can be "confident of this very thing, that he which hath begun a good work in you will perform it until the day of Jesus Christ" (Phil. 1:6). So let me ask you this question: Is God finished with you yet?

The good news is that you're not in this all alone. God is with you every step of the way. One of my favorite Scripture verses says it best: "'For I know the plans I have for you,' declares the LORD, 'plans to prosper you and not to harm you, plans to give you hope and a future'" (Jer. 29:11 NIV).

Be confident and receive God's momentum for your life.

Part 1

LOOKING INWARD

NUGGET #1

A Diamond Is a Hunk of Coal That Stuck to Its Job and Made Good Under Pressure

Growing up in the late 1950s and 1960s, most of my friends and I had a popular toy that was a blow-up figure with a weighted bottom. The figure could be a clown, a cowboy, or some evil character. I had a clown. It was fun to punch. I'd watch it fall over and then spring right back to attention. No matter how hard I punched or what technique I used, this fun toy came back for more. Today this toy teaches me a lesson: we may get knocked over, but the key to bouncing back and not staying down is having the right foundation.

A good prayer to pray when you feel like giving up is, "Lord, give me the determination and tenacity of a weed." I don't like weeds, but I have to admire their resolve. A great oak is only a little nut that held its ground. "Somebody is sitting in the shade today because someone long ago planted a tree" (Warren Buffett). "These troubles and sufferings of ours are, after all, quite small and won't last very long. Yet this short time of distress will result in God's richest blessing upon us forever and ever" (2 Cor. 4:17 TLB). Most of us take hold of opportunity, but we let go of it too soon.

> Many people fail in life because they believe in the adage "If you don't succeed at one thing right away, try something else." But success eludes those who follow such advice. The dreams that have come true did so because people stuck to their ambitions. They refused to be discouraged. They never let disappointment get the upper hand. Challenges only spurred them on to greater efforts.
>
> Don B. Owens Jr.

You'll be judged by what you finish, not by what you start. If you don't see results right away, don't worry. God doesn't pay by the week, He pays at the end.

All great achievements require time and tenacity. "The reward for those who persevere far exceeds the pain that must precede the victory" (Ted Engstrom). It is not success that God rewards but faithfulness in doing His will. Be persevering—it may be the last key on the ring that opens the door. Hanging on one second longer than your competition makes you a winner. Become famous for finishing important, difficult tasks.

If you're tempted to stop, just think of Brahms. He took seven long years to compose his famous lullaby because he kept falling asleep at the piano—*just kidding*! But it really did take him that long to finish. I agree with Woodrow Wilson when he said, "I would rather fail in a cause that will ultimately succeed than succeed in a cause that will ultimately fail." Nearly all failures result from people quitting too soon. "And let us not get tired of doing what is right, for after a while we will reap a harvest of blessing if we don't get discouraged and give up" (Gal. 6:9 TLB). It takes the hammer of persistence to drive the nail of success.

Many of life's failures were people who didn't realize how close they were to success when they gave up. Harriet Beecher Stowe wrote, "When you get into a tight place and everything goes against you, until it seems as though you could not hold on a minute longer, never give up then, for that is just the time and place that the tide will turn." The lowest ebb is the turn of the tide.

You uncover opportunity by applying persistence to possibilities. When you get right down to the root meaning of the word *succeed*, you find it simply means to persevere and follow through. Any diamond will tell you it was just a hunk of coal that stuck to its job and made good under pressure.

The road to success runs uphill, so don't expect to break any speed records. Impatience is costly. Your greatest mistakes will happen because of impatience. Most people fail simply because they're impatient and they cannot join the beginning with the end. Keep patiently doing God's will if you want Him to do for you all He has promised.

> The determined soul will do more with a rusty monkey wrench than a loafer will accomplish with all the tools in a mechanic's shop.
>
> Rupert Hughs

The power to hold on in spite of everything, to endure—this is the winner's quality. To endure is greater than to dare. The difference between the impossible and the possible lies simply in a person's determination.

NUGGET
#2

When You're Trying to Be
Like Someone Else,
the Best You Can Ever Be
Is Number Two

You and I are born equal but also different. Do you want to stand out in the world? Then be you. Be who you really are. This is the first step toward becoming better than what you are now.

> No man could be ideally successful until he has found his place. Like a locomotive, he is strong on the track, but weak anywhere else.
>
> Orison Marden

Choose to become yourself. Avoid following the crowd. Be an engine, not a caboose. "It is better to fail in originality than to succeed in imitation" (Herman Melville). Average people would rather be wrong than different. We relinquish three-fourths of ourselves in order to be like other people. Conformity is the jailer of satisfaction and the enemy of growth. Did you know you're destined to be different? Dare to be different and follow your own star.

"Be yourself. Who else is better qualified?" (Frank Giblin). Ask yourself these two questions: (1) If I try to be like someone else, who will be like me? (2) If I'm not me, who will I be? The more you develop *your* potential, the less you'll become like someone else.

Trying to be like someone else is self-defeating. One of your main purposes in life is to give birth to yourself. As long as you are trying to be like someone else, the best you can ever be is *number two*.

Upon completing a highly dangerous tightrope walk over Niagara Falls in appalling wind and rain, the Great Zumbrati was met by an enthusiastic supporter, who urged him to make a return trip, this time pushing a wheelbarrow, which the spectator had thoughtfully brought along.

The Great Zumbrati was reluctant, given the terrible conditions, but the supporter pressed him. "You can do it—I know you can," he urged.

"You really believe I can do it?" asked Zumbrati.

"Yes—definitely—you can do it," the supporter gushed.

"Okay," said Zumbrati, "get in the wheelbarrow . . ."

What you think you see in another person's life is not reality. You can't reach your destiny by taking another person's road. When you walk only where you see another's tracks, you'll make no new discoveries. "Do not follow where the path may lead—go instead where there's no path and leave a trail" (unknown). "God has given each of us the ability to do certain things well" (Rom. 12:6 TLB).

"Don't let the world around you squeeze you into its own mold, but let God remake you so that your whole attitude of mind is changed" (Rom. 12:2 Phillips). "The more you are like yourself, the less you are like anyone else" (Walt Disney). You're like a tree; you must put forth the fruit created in you.

Don't be common. The common goes nowhere. You must be uncommon to be a champion. Your responsibility is not to *remake* yourself but to *make* the absolute best of what God made. Don't compromise yourself . . . it's all you've got. "Almost every man wastes part of his life in attempts to display qualities he does not possess" (Samuel Johnson). Don't let your life be a continual struggle to be what you are not and to do what you're not supposed to do.

You're an unprecedented miracle. You're as God made you, and since He's satisfied, you should be too.

NUGGET #3

People Say They Want Riches When What They Need Is Fulfillment of a Purpose

The world makes room for a person of purpose. Her words and actions demonstrate she *knows* where she's going. You're built to conquer circumstances, solve problems, and attain goals. You'll find no real satisfaction or happiness in life without obstacles to conquer, goals to achieve, and a purpose to accomplish. People may say they want money; what they really need is satisfaction. Happiness comes when you squander yourself for a purpose.

In your heart is a sleeping lion. No person alive can completely shun his or her destiny. Be on a mission. Have a definite sense of direction and purpose for your life. Successful lives are motivated by dynamic purpose. God can only bless your plan and direct you in accomplishing it if you have one. Strong convictions precede great actions.

As soon as you resign yourself to fate, your resignation is promptly accepted. You don't have a fate, you have a destiny. When you look into the future, it's so bright it will make you squint. "It's never too late to be what you might have been" (George Eliot).

"More men fail through lack of purpose than lack of talent" (Billy Sunday). If your method is hit or miss, you'll usually miss. "If you're not sure where you are going, you'll probably end up someplace else" (Robert F. Mager). Too many people don't know where they're going, but they're on their way. Growth for the sake of growth is the ideology of the cancer cell. Go forward with purpose.

> The only thing some people do is grow older.
>
> Ed Howe

Lord Chesterfield wrote, "Firmness of purpose is one of the most necessary sinews of character and one of the best instruments of success. Without it, genius wastes its efforts in a maze of inconsistencies." The man who has no direction is the slave of his circumstances. The poorest man is not he who is without a cent but he who is without a purpose. There's good news for each of us in walking out our purpose. Jesus said, "My yoke is easy and my burden is light" (Matt. 11:30).

"If you don't have a vision for your life, then you probably haven't focused in on anything" (Dr. David Burns). In the absence of vision there can be no clear and constant focus. When your purpose is clear, decisions become more obvious. "When you discover your mission, you will feel its demand. It will fill you with enthusiasm and a burning desire to get to work on it" (W. Clement Stone).

NUGGET
#4

Don't Live
Within Your Means

It doesn't happen often, but while I was writing this book, I believe the Lord awakened me in the middle of the night. I felt Him leading me to write a nugget titled "Don't Live Within Your Means." Even though it was 4:50 a.m., I was so excited that I woke my wife and began to "preach" to her about it for several minutes. (She said the idea was great, but she really needed her sleep!)

What do I believe God meant by this? I believe He wants us to act bigger, believe larger, associate higher, and (with His help) do more than we can ask or think. Your outlook determines your outcome. If God is your partner . . . make your plans BIG.

I'm not encouraging you to go wild, to have no boundaries, or to be reckless. Certainly we should spend within our means—but not *live* there. Talk with people smarter than you. Listen to those more spiritual than you. Ask questions of those more successful than you. Lend a hand to those less fortunate than you. Don't stay where you are.

I sincerely believe many people who think they're frugal aren't really frugal. Rather, they're full of fear. The label of frugality, balance, or conservativeness is often a mask to cover up a person's deep-rooted fear. Don't make such thorough plans for rainy days that you don't enjoy today's sunshine.

When you live only within your means, you can't live by faith. If you aren't living by faith, you can't please God, for "without faith it is impossible to please him" (Heb. 11:6). Abandon altogether the search for security. "Only the insecure strive for security" (Wayne Dyer). If you're just trying to earn a living, you'll forget how to live.

I've heard this saying most of my life: "Whom God calls, He equips. Whom He equips, He anoints to do the job." No matter what level of your ability, God has equipped you with more potential than you can possibly use in your lifetime. Don't let the future be a time when you wish you'd done what you aren't doing now.

If the shoe fits . . . don't wear it. If you do, you're not allowing room for growth. Webster knew all about the ineffectiveness of "living within your means." When you look up the word *means* in his dictionary, it tells you to see the word *average*. So when you decide to live within your means, you're deciding to live an average life.

NUGGET
#5

If You're Not Failing, You're Not Growing

An inspirational speaker began his seminar by holding up a twenty-dollar bill. He asked the two hundred people in the room, "Who would like this twenty-dollar bill?"

Hands started going up.

"I am going to give this twenty dollars to one of you," he said. "But first, let me do this," and he proceeded to crumple the bill.

He then asked, "Who still wants it?"

Still the hands were in the air.

"Well," he continued, "what if I do this?" And he dropped it on the ground and started to grind it into the floor with his shoe.

He picked it up, now all crumpled and dirty. "Now who still wants it?" Still the hands went into the air.

"My friends, you have all learned a very valuable lesson. No matter what I did to the money, you still wanted it because it did not decrease in value. It was still worth twenty dollars."

Many times in our lives, we are dropped, crumpled, and ground into the dirt by the decisions we make and the circumstances that come our way. We feel as though we are worthless. But no matter what has happened or what will happen, you will never lose your value.

We all make mistakes—especially those who do things. Failure is often the first necessary step toward success. If we don't take the risk of failing, we won't get the chance to succeed. When we're trying, we're winning. To fail is the natural consequence of trying. Babe Ruth, one of the great home-run hitters but also the all-time strikeout leader, always said, "Never let the fear of striking out get in your way."

Stop trying to be perfect. When you have a serious decision to make, tell yourself firmly you are going to make it. Don't expect it will be a perfect one. I love the wisdom of Winston Churchill: "The maxim 'nothing avails but perfection' may be spelled P-A-R-A-L-Y-S-I-S." The pursuit of excellence is gratifying and healthy; the pursuit of perfection is frustrating, neurotic, and a terrible waste of time.

> I don't like these cold, precise, perfect people who, in order not to speak wrong, never speak at all, and in order not to do wrong, never do anything.
>
> Henry Ward Beecher

The fact is, you're like a tea bag. You won't know your own strength until you've been through some hot water. Failure is something we can avoid only by saying nothing, doing nothing, and being nothing. "Remember, there are two benefits of failure. First, if you do fail, you learn what doesn't work; and second, the failure gives you an opportunity to try a new approach" (Roger Von Oech).

Some defeats are only installments to victory. "Even a mistake may turn out to be the one thing necessary to a worthwhile achievement" (Henry Ford). Some people learn from their mistakes; some never recover from them. Learn how to fail intelligently. Develop success from failure.

Mistakes and failure are two of the surest stepping-stones to success. No other element can do so much for a person who is willing to study them and to make the most out of them. "Most people think of success and failure as opposites, but they are actually both products of the same process" (Roger Von Oech). Your season of failure is the best time for sowing your seeds of success.

Successful people are not afraid to fail. They go from failure to failure . . . until at last success is theirs. The best way to accelerate your success is to double your failure rate. The law of failure is one of the most powerful of all success laws.

> No matter what mistakes you have made—no matter how you've messed things up—you can still make a new beginning. The person who fully realizes this suffers less from the shock and pain of failure and sooner gets off to a new beginning.
>
> Norman Vincent Peale

"When you stumble today, pick yourself up tomorrow. That's what tomorrows are for" (Janet Collins). Often just before the big success . . . comes apparent failure and discouragement. "I hope someday to have so much of what the world calls success, that people will ask me, 'What's your secret?' And I will tell them, 'I just get up again when I fall down'" (Paul Harvey).

The greatest mistake you can make in life is to continually fear you will make one. "Don't be afraid to fail. Don't waste energy trying to cover up failure. If you're not failing, you're not growing" (H. Stanley Judd). When successful people stop growing and learning, it's usually because they have become less and less willing to risk failure. "Failure should be our teacher, not our undertaker. Failure is delay, not defeat. It is a temporary detour, not a dead-end street" (William A. Ward).

If you are made of the right stuff, a hard fall results in a sky-high bounce. A life spent making mistakes is not only more honorable but also more useful than a life spent doing nothing.

NUGGET #6

Constantly Frustrate Tradition with Your Creativity and Imagination

A small boy is sent to bed by his father. Five minutes later: "Da-ad . . ."

"What?"

"I'm thirsty. Can you bring me a drink of water?"

"No. You had your chance. Lights out."

Five minutes later: "Da-aaaad . . ."

"WHAT?"

"I'm THIRSTY. Can I have a drink of water?"

"I told you NO! If you ask again, I'll have to spank you!"

Five minutes later: "Daaaa-aaaad . . ."

"WHAT!"

"When you come in to spank me, can you bring a drink of water?"

It's fun to continually frustrate tradition with your creativity and imagination. "The opportunities of man are limited only by his imagination. But so few have imagination that there are ten thousand fiddlers to one composer" (Charles Kettering).

Your dreams are a preview to your greatness. All people who have achieved great things have been dreamers. Those who do most, dream most. A shallow thinker seldom makes a deep impression. We act, or fail to act, not because of *determination*, as is so commonly believed, but because of *imagination*. Only a person who sees the invisible can do the impossible.

Someone once said, "Ideas are like rabbits. You get a couple and learn how to handle them, and pretty soon you have a dozen." You'll get more out of every part of your life if you stay incurably curious. "The important thing is to not stop questioning. Never lose a holy curiosity" (Albert Einstein). Dexter Yager says, "Don't let anybody steal your dream."

God gave us a world unfinished so we might share in the joy and satisfaction of creation. "Creativity has been built into every one of us; it's part of our design. Each of us lives less of the life God intended for us when we choose not to live out the creative powers we possess" (Ted Engstrom).

> I'm a big fan of dreams. Unfortunately, dreams are the first casualty in life—people seem to give them up quicker than anything for a "reality."
>
> Kevin Costner

Realistic people with practical aims are rarely as realistic or practical in the long-run of life as the dreamers who pursue their dreams.

Hans Selye

Stop and daydream once in a while. You need to let your imagination roam and give it a chance to breathe. It's never too late for you to start thinking more creatively. Often it's just a lack of imagination that keeps you from your potential. Thinking of new ideas is like shaving: if you don't do it every day, you're a bum. Have a constant flow of new, exciting, powerful ideas on which you act immediately.

What you need is an idea. Be brave enough to live creatively.

NUGGET #7

Get Ahead During the Time Others Waste

Don't be a person who says, "Ready. Aim . . . aim . . . aim . . . aim . . ." As fast as each opportunity presents itself, use it! No matter how small an opportunity may be, use it! Do the thing you have to do when it ought to be done whether you like it or not. "He who hesitates misses the green light, gets bumped in the rear, and loses his parking space" (Herbert Prochnow).

One of the deceptions of an unproductive life is that this present day is not important. Every day comes bearing its own gifts. Untie the ribbons, tear into the wrapping, and open them up. Write it on your heart: *every day is the best day of the year.* "This is the day that the Lord has made; let us rejoice and be glad in it" (Ps. 118:24 NRSV).

By the time the fool has learned to play the game, the players have dispersed and the rules have changed. Don't find yourself striking when the iron is cold. Instead, scratch opportunity where it itches. "Walk while ye have the light, lest darkness come upon you" (John 12:35). Life is made of constant calls to action.

"Successful leaders have the courage to take action while others hesitate" (John Maxwell). You never know what you can do until you try. Remember, the moment you say, "I give up," someone else is seeing the same situation and saying, "My, what a great opportunity." The fact is that no opportunity is ever lost; someone else just picks up the ones you missed. A secret of success in life is to be ready for opportunity when it comes. Ability is nothing without opportunity.

Time flies. It's up to you to be the pilot. "Everything comes to him who hustles while he waits" (Thomas Edison). It's been my observation that most successful people get ahead during the time others waste. A secret of success is to do something else in the meantime. Make quick use of the moment.

It is later than you think. Be ready now. God's alarm clock has no snooze button. It doesn't do any good to stand up and take notice if you sit down as soon as opportunity passes by. Look at it . . . size it up . . . make a decision. You postpone your life when you can't make up your mind. "If you wait for perfect conditions you will never get anything done. . . . Keep on sowing your seed, for you never know which will grow—perhaps it all will" (Eccles. 11:4, 6 TLB).

William Ward has this recipe for success: "Study while others are sleeping; work while others are loafing; prepare while others are playing; and dream while others are wishing." There is no time like the present and no present like time. Those who take advantage of their advantage get the advantage in this world. Don't find yourself at the end of your life saying, "What a wonderful life I've had! I only wish I had realized and appreciated it sooner."

NUGGET
#8

Get Out of the Middle of the Road

Your destiny is not a matter of chance; it's a matter of choice. Many people have the right aims in life—they just never get around to pulling the trigger. When you determine what you want, you have made the most important decision in your life. You have to know what you want in order to attain it.

"Commit your way to the LORD, trust also in Him, and He will do it" (Ps. 37:5 NASB). If we are faithful, God will take care of our successes. Peace is the result of a deliberate decision, an adjustment of your life to the will of God. Guidance means I can count on God. Commitment means God can count on me.

"Not to decide is to decide" (Harvey Cox). Weeds grow lushly in the soil of indecision. Get out of the middle of the road. Standing in the middle of the road is very dangerous; you can get knocked down by traffic going both directions. The train of failure usually runs on the track of indecision. Because of indecision, one can die before one is actually dead.

> Indecision is debilitating; it feeds upon itself; it is, one might say, habit forming. Not only that, but it is contagious; it transmits itself to others.
>
> H. A. Hopf

"There is a fine difference of perspective between getting involved and being committed. In ham and eggs, the chicken is involved, but the pig is committed" (John Alan Price). Until you're committed, there's hesitancy, the chance to draw back, always ineffectiveness. "I will" is a slogan for an exciting, productive life.

You must choose between boredom and decisions. Don't be like a wheelbarrow—going no farther than others push you. The weak are always forced to decide between alternatives others have set before them and they have not chosen themselves. "Never complain about what you permit" (Mike Murdock).

You're where you are today because you've chosen to be there. Reality forms around a commitment, and one person with commitment always accomplishes more than a hundred people with mere interest. Commitment is what transforms an idea into a reality.

Be decisive, even if it means you'll sometimes be wrong. The key to your future is that you can still choose. "Keep thy heart with all diligence; for out of it are the issues of life" (Prov. 4:23). What you commit yourself to be will change you from what you are into what you can be.

NUGGET
#9

What You See Depends Mainly on What You Look For

The reason many people don't get answers from God is the same reason a thief doesn't find a policeman: they are running away. How we position ourselves in life makes all the difference. To one person the world is desolate, dull, and empty. To another the same world looks rich, interesting, and full of meaning. The choice is up to you. It's like how a twenty-dollar bill looks so big when it goes to church and so little when it goes out for groceries.

If you look at life the wrong way, there's always cause for alarm. Most people complain because roses have thorns.

Instead, be thankful thorns have roses. What you see depends mainly on what you look for.

A young man was getting ready to graduate from college. For many months he had admired a beautiful sports car in a dealer's showroom. Knowing his father could well afford it, he told him that was all he wanted.

As graduation day approached, the young man awaited signs that his father had purchased the car. Finally, on the morning of his graduation, his father called him into his private study. His father told him how proud he was to have such a fine son and how much he loved him. He handed his son a beautifully wrapped gift box. Curious but somewhat disappointed, the young man opened the box and found a lovely, leather-bound Bible. Angrily, he raised his voice at his father and said, "With all your money you give me a Bible?" and stormed out of the house, leaving the holy book.

Many years passed and the young man was very successful in business. He had a beautiful home and a wonderful family. But he realized his father was now very old and thought perhaps he should go to him. He had not seen him since that graduation day. Before he could make arrangements, the man received a telegram telling him his father had passed away and willed all of his possessions to him. He needed to come home immediately and take care of things. When he arrived at his father's house, sudden sadness and regret filled his heart.

He began to search his father's important papers and saw the still-new Bible, just as he had left it years ago. Through tears, he opened the Bible and began to turn the pages. As he read those words, a car key dropped from an envelope taped behind the Bible. It had a tag with a dealer's name, the same dealer who had the sports car he had desired. On the tag was the date of his graduation and the words PAID IN FULL.

How many times do we miss God's blessings because they are not packaged as we expected?

Position yourself to *receive*, not *resist*. How you see things on the outside depends on how things are on the inside of you. "Any fact facing us is not as important as our attitude toward it, for that determines our success or failure" (Norman Vincent Peale). "You and I do not see things as they are. We see things as we are" (Herb Cohen). Develop the hunter's approach, the outlook that wherever you go there are ideas waiting to be discovered. When you are positioned right, opportunity presents itself.

Opportunity can be missed if you're broadcasting when you should be tuning in. When opportunity knocks, some people object to the interruption. "One of the greatest and most comforting truths is that when one door opens, another closes, but often we look so long and regretfully upon the closed door that we do not see the one that is open for us" (Anonymous).

See success where others see only failure. Expect something good to happen. That expectation will energize your dreams and give them momentum. You'll often find life responds to your outlook. We go where our vision is. Life is mostly a matter of expectation.

You'll gain the advantage by doing things before they need to be done—positioning yourself ahead of time. Enduring success is found when you travel in advance of the crowd. I believe one of the major benefits of reading the Bible is that it teaches us how to respond in advance to many of life's challenges and opportunities.

Dig a well before you're thirsty. Plant a seed before you're hungry. The trouble with the future for most people is it arrives before they are ready for it. Positioning yourself to receive causes you to be ready. The most important question is, *Are you ready?*

NUGGET
#10

When You Excuse Yourself, You Accuse Yourself

Ninety-nine percent of failures come from people who have a habit of making excuses.

George Washington Carver

You're never a failure until you begin to blame somebody else. Stop blaming others. You'll find that when you become good at making excuses you won't be good at anything else. Excuses are the tools a person without purpose or vision uses to build great monuments of emptiness.

Most people could learn from their mistakes if they weren't so busy denying and defending them. "It seems to me these days that people who admit they're wrong get a lot further than people who prove they're right" (Deryl Pfizer). What poison is to food alibis are to a productive life. "Work brings profit; talk brings poverty" (Prov. 14:23 TLB). "Some men have thousands of reasons why they can't do what they want to do, when all they really need is one reason why they can" (Willis Whitney). Find a reason why you can.

One of the biggest alibis is regret. Don't leave any regrets on the field—give your all in the game of life. "The most valuable thing I have learned from life is to regret nothing" (Somerset Maugham). Eliminate all your regrets. The masses of people live lives of quiet regret. "Regret is an appalling waste of energy; you can't build on it. It's only good for wallowing in" (Catherine Mansfield). The truth is, a thousand regrets do not pay one debt. Live your life so your tombstone reads "No regrets."

A winner who makes a mistake says, "I was wrong." A loser who makes a mistake says, "It wasn't my fault." Do you admit and say, "I was wrong"? Or do you say, "It wasn't my fault"? A winner explains, a loser explains away.

Idle people lack no excuses. The word *can't* really means you won't try. The word *can't* is the worst word ever written or spoken, doing more harm than slander or lies. *Can't* is the worst excuse and the biggest enemy of success.

We have many reasons for failure but not a single excuse. "Excuses always replace progress" (Ralph Waldo Emerson). "In everything you do, stay away from complaining and arguing so that no one can speak a word of blame against you" (Phil. 2:14–15 TLB). Alibis and excuses should be cremated, not embalmed. Excuses are of no avail before God.

The best years of your life are the ones in which you decide your problems are your own. You don't blame them on your mother, the ecology, or the President. You realize that you control your own destiny.

Albert Ellis

We should live our lives like Florence Nightingale when she said, "I attribute my success to this: I never gave or took an excuse."

NUGGET
#11

Bite Off More
Than You Can Chew

Don't do anything that doesn't require faith. The key to momentum is always having something to look forward to in faith. We live by faith, or we don't really live at all. Either we venture or we vegetate.

What's needed is more people who specialize in the impossible. This year's success was last year's impossibility. "Faith is not trying to believe something regardless of the evidence. Faith is daring to do something regardless of the consequence" (Sherwood Eddy).

Phillip Brooks suggested we pray this way: "Do not pray for easy lives. Pray to be stronger men. Do not pray for tasks equal to your power. Pray for power equal to your tasks." Jesus said to you and me, "I am come that they might have life, and that they might have it more abundantly" (John 10:10). Never be afraid to do what God tells you to do. "Shoot for the moon. Even if you miss it, you will land among the stars" (Les Brown). You're like a rubber band. You must be stretched in order to be effective.

You can only accomplish in proportion to what you attempt. The reason why so little is accomplished is because so little is attempted. Never say never. You have to think big to be big. "It is not because things are difficult that we do not dare; it is because we do not dare that things are difficult" (Seneca).

The impossible: what nobody can do until somebody does.

The fact is, it's fun to do the impossible. It's when we play it safe that we create a world of utmost insecurity. So look at things . . . as they can be.

You don't tap the resources of God until you attempt the impossible. Risk is part of God's plan for you. "I can do everything God asks me to with the help of Christ who gives me the strength and the power" (Phil. 4:13 TLB). "Mediocre minds usually dismiss anything which reaches beyond their own understanding" (Rochefoucauld). Even a coward can praise Christ, but it takes a person of courage to follow Him.

Progress always involves risk. You can't steal second base and keep your foot on first. "We do not need more intellectual power, we need more spiritual power. We do not need more things that are seen, we need more of the things that are unseen" (Calvin Coolidge). He who does not dare will not get his share. Unless you enter the beehive, you can't take the honey.

Look for ways to flex your risk muscle. Everyone has a risk muscle, and you keep it in the proper shape by experimenting and trying new things. "People who take risks are the people you'll lose against" (John Scully). "The people who are really failures are the people who set their standards so low, keep the bar at such a safe level, that they never run the risk of failure" (Robert Schuller).

A great ship always asks for deep water. When you dare for nothing you should hope for nothing. God wants us to bite off more than we can chew, to live by faith and not by sight.

NUGGET
#12

Questions

In the first four books of the New Testament, Jesus asks over 150 questions! I know. I counted them. Here's a man who's known as "the Answer" and He's asking all the questions. Why?

I've always observed this characteristic of productive and successful people—they ask good questions. I noticed that whether or not these people took action was greatly influenced by the questions they asked. I observed that as they asked more outstanding questions, their focus in life changed and improved. They automatically became more productive!

Life's most important answers can be found in asking the right questions. So consider these:

- Both enthusiasm and pessimism are contagious. How much of each do you spread?

- If someone were to pay you a hundred dollars for each kind word you spoke and collect fifty dollars for each unkind word, would you be rich or poor?

- Are you a creature of circumstance or a creator of circumstance?

- Are you ready for your opportunity when it comes?

- Do you make others feel bigger or smaller when they're around you?

- Are you spending your life answering questions nobody is asking?

- Ten years from today, what will you wish you had done right now?

- If you have God's promise for something, isn't that enough?

- Why worry when you can pray?

- How old is your attitude?

- Are you ready?

- Do you acquire the doubts of others?

- Are you willing to follow the truth no matter where it leads?

- How much have fear and worry about things that never happened cost you?

- Do you go *through* a problem, or do you try to go *around* it and never get *past* it?

- Do you say, "There ought to be a better way to do it"? Or do you say, "That's the way it's always been done"?

- Are you deliberately planning to be less than you're capable of being? If not you, then who? If not now, then when?

- Are you willing to give up what you have in order to become what you can be?

- What do you believe in the deepest part of your being?

- What is the first small step you can take to get moving?

- Are you thinking of security or opportunity?

- Do you look at the horizon and see an opportunity, or do you look into the distance and fear a problem?

- Do you put off until tomorrow the things you've already put off until today?

- Has failure gone to your head?

- Does your reach exceed your grasp?

- "Do you spend the first six days of each week sowing wild oats, then go to church on Sunday and pray for a crop failure?" (Fred Allen)

- Are you traveling or going somewhere?

- Are you always ready to live but never living?

- Do you see difficulties in every opportunity, or do you see opportunities in every difficulty?

- How many people of great potential have you known? Where on earth did they all go?

- Are you content with failure?

- "What progress are you standing in the way of?" (Tim Redmond)

- Does God seem far away? If so, guess who moved. He's never more than a prayer or praise away.

- "Is anything too hard for the LORD?" (Gen 18:14)

- Do you still believe that anything is possible? Or have you come to believe that nothing is possible?

God is never too big or too little for your problems. He is able. No matter what area of your life you want to improve, there are questions you can ask that will provide you with the right answers. What are the questions that are shaping your life?

NUGGET #13

Change, but Don't Stop

When you're through changing, you're through. Most people fail in life because they're unwilling to make changes. But correction and change always result in fruit.

People are divided into three classes: (1) those who are unchangeable, (2) those who are changeable, and (3) those who cause change.

> Change is always hardest for the man who's in a rut. For he has scaled down his living to that which he can handle comfortably and welcomes no change or challenge that would lift him up.
>
> C. Neil Strait

If you find yourself in a hole . . . stop digging. When things go wrong—don't go with them. Stubbornness and unwillingness to change are the energy of fools.

"He that will not apply new remedies must expect new evils" (Francis Bacon). "I will instruct you (says the Lord) and guide you along the best pathway for your life; I will advise you and watch your progress" (Ps. 32:8 TLB). God never closes one door without opening another one. We must be willing to change in order to walk through that new door.

In prayer we learn to change. Prayer is one of the most changing experiences you'll ever know. You can't pray and stay the same.

Playing it safe is really the most unsafe thing in the world. You *can't* stand still. You must go forward and be open to the adjustments God has for you. The unhappiest people are those who fear change. Everyone goes through changes, whether they want to or not. Nothing stays the same.

Before: Acid rock
Now: Acid reflux

Before: Moving to California because it's cool
Now: Moving to California because it's warm

Before: Trying to look like Marlon Brando or Liz Taylor
Now: Trying NOT to look like Marlon Brando or Liz Taylor

Before: Hoping for a BMW
Now: Hoping for a BM

Before: Going to a new, hip joint
Now: Receiving a new hip joint

Before: Rolling Stones
Now: Kidney stones

Before: Being called into the principal's office
Now: Calling the principal's office

Before: Fight the system
Now: Upgrade the system

Before: Disco
Now: Costco

Before: Parents begging you to get your hair cut
Now: Children begging you to get their heads shaved

Before: Passing the drivers' test
Now: Passing the vision test

Before: "Whatever"
Now: Depends

Change is here to stay. You can't make an omelet without breaking some eggs. Mix things up, scramble the norm, and stir the pot! Accomplishment automatically results in change. One change makes way for the next, giving you the opportunity to grow. You must change to master change.

You've got to be open to change, because just when you think you're ready to graduate from the school of experience, somebody thinks up a new course. Decide to be willing to experience change. If you can figure out when to stand firm and when to bend, you've got it made. We can become nervous because of incessant change, but we would be frightened if the change were stopped.

Blessed is the one who can adjust to a set of circumstances without surrendering conviction. Open your arms to change, but don't let go of your values. The majority of people meet with failure because they lack persistence in developing new ideas and plans to take the place of those that failed. Your growth depends on your willingness to experience change. Welcome change as a friend.

NUGGET
#14

It's Passion That Persuades

The starting point of all accomplishment is desire. Keep this in mind: feeble desires bring feeble results just as a small amount of fire makes a small amount of heat. Be passionate about your life, and act from your passion. The more energy you apply to any task, the more you will have to apply to the next task. "Whatsoever thy hand findeth to do, do it with thy might" (Eccles. 9:10).

Desire is the planting of your seed. Deep desire creates not only its own opportunities but also its own talents. Attitudes alter abilities. If you have the desire, distance doesn't matter. "A strong passion for any object will insure success, for the desire of the end will point out the means" (William Hazlitt).

The trouble with many educated people is that learning goes to their heads and not to their hearts. Does the path you're traveling capture your heart? God has put you in this world to pour your heart into something. You will only be remembered in life for your passions. Find something that consumes you. A belief is not just an idea a person possesses; it's an idea that possesses a person. "Whatsoever ye do, do it heartily, as to the Lord, and not unto men" (Col. 3:23). Learn to be comfortable with being enthusiastic.

Every time zeal and passion are discussed, someone brings up *balance*. Balance can be a tremendous virtue, but the immediate neighbors of balance are apathy and weakness. If the truth were known, being balanced is usually an excuse for being lukewarm, indifferent, or neutral. Indifference, lukewarmness, and neutrality are always attached to failure.

Enthusiasm can achieve in one day what can never happen by reason alone. "Above all else, guard your affections. For they influence everything else in your life" (Prov. 4:23 TLB). "Perhaps the greatest discovery of this century is that if you change your attitude, you can change your life" (William James).

"Believing is seeing. It's much more effective than the old notion that seeing is believing" (Terrence Deal). Love the thing you do and you will keep doing bigger and better things.

NUGGET #15

If You Don't Do It, You Don't Really Believe It

People judge you by your actions, not your intentions. You may have a heart of gold, but so does a hard-boiled egg.

Anonymous

A thousand words will not leave so lasting an impression as one deed. Action is the natural fruit of direction. Follow good intentions with appropriate actions. "If ye *know* these things, happy are ye if you *do* them" (John 13:17, italics added).

Prayer should never be an excuse for inaction. Sometimes, I believe the Lord speaks to us like He spoke to Moses when He said, "Quit praying and get the people moving! Forward march!" (Exod. 14:15 TLB). If you don't take action, you don't *really* believe it. Most prayers are only going to be answered when you attach action to them. Decide in advance to act on the answers to your prayers.

Some people spend their whole life searching for what's right, but they can't seem to find any time to practice it. "Remember, too, that knowing what is right to do and then not doing it is sin" (James 4:17 TLB). Your life story is not written with a pen but with your actions. To *do* nothing is the way to *be* nothing.

There is no idleness without a thousand troubles.

Welsh proverb

The devil's number-one hope is not an active sinner but an inactive Christian. "The devil tempts some, but an idle man tempts the devil" (English proverb). Be sure to keep busy doing what's right so the devil may always find you occupied.

Action subdues fear. When we challenge our fears, we master them. When we wrestle with our problems, they lose their grip on us. When we dare to confront the things that scare us, we open the door to our liberty.

Momentum doesn't just happen. "The common conception is that motivation leads to action, but the reverse is true—action precedes motivation" (Robert McKain). "Don't wait to be motivated. Take the bull by the horns until you have him screaming for mercy" (Michael Cadena).

Laziness is a load. Nothing is more exhausting than searching for easy ways to make a living. Expectation is the idle man's income. Laziness keeps on and on, but soon enough it arrives at poverty. We are weakest when we try to get something for nothing. "Hard work brings prosperity; playing around brings poverty" (Prov. 28:19 TLB).

A person of words and not of deeds is like a flower bed full of weeds. Don't let weeds grow around your dreams. To only dream of the person you would like to be is to waste the person you are. Some people dream of great accomplishments, while others stay awake and do them. Henry Ford commented, "You can't build a reputation on what you're going to do." "Shun idleness. It is a rust that attaches itself to the most brilliant of metals" (Voltaire).

Be a combination of a carrier pigeon and a woodpecker: don't just carry the message, but also knock on the door.

NUGGET
#16

You Cannot Find
Until You Define

Opportunity is all around you. What matters is where you put your focus. Ask yourself this question every day: *Where should my focus be?* Where you focus your attention, you create strength and momentum.

These are the characteristics of momentum: (1) it is single-minded; (2) it is unwavering in the pursuit of a goal; (3) it has passion that knows no limits; (4) it demands a concentrated intensity and a definite sense of destiny; and, most of all, (5) it has a boundless vision and commitment to excellence.

Concentration is the key that opens the door to accomplishment. "The first law of success is concentration—to bend all your energies to one point and go directly to that point, looking neither to the right nor to the left" (William Mathews). The most successful people have always been people with concentration. They struck their blows in one place until they accomplished their purpose. They have one specific idea, one steady aim, and one single, concentrated purpose.

What a great abyss between some people's dreams and the results they achieve! Bring together all the options of your ability and focus them on one point.

There are two quick ways to disaster: taking nobody's advice and taking everybody's advice. Learn to say no to the good so you can say yes to the best. A. P. Goethe said there are three qualifications for success:

1. A big wastebasket—you must know what to eliminate.
2. You must know what to preserve.
3. You must know when to say no, for developing the power to say no gives us the capacity to say yes.

We accomplish things by directing our desires, not by ignoring them. What an immense power you have over your life when you possess distinct aims. Your words, the tone of your voice, your dress, and your very motions change and improve when you begin to live for a reason.

Don't be a person who is uncertain about the future and hazy about the present. Stay in the groove without making it a rut. Make something your specialty. Even God, who is God, cannot please everyone, so don't you try. You cannot find until you define. To finish the race, stay on the track.

I'm astonished at the aimlessness of most people's lives and how easily they delegate the direction of their lives to others. "Learn to define yourself, to content yourself with some specific thing and some definite work; dare to be what you really are, and to learn to accept with good grace all that you are not" (Anonymous).

NUGGET
#17

Impatience Is One Big "Get-Ahead-Ache"

"Time sure changes things," an airline passenger told his companion. "When I was a boy I used to sit in a flat-bottom rowboat and fish in the lake down there below us. Every time a plane flew over, I'd look up and wish I were in it. Now I look down and wish I were fishing."

Timing makes all the difference. How important is it? Theodore Roosevelt said, "Nine tenths of wisdom is being wise in time." Wise people are very intentional about being at the right place at the right time with the right idea or action.

The fact that you're reading this book shows you want to grow—to get somewhere important. Like most of us, you want to get there as fast as you can. But keep in mind that being too swift is as untimely as being too slow. The situation that seems urgent seldom is. Haste slows every dream and opens the door to premature failure. "The more haste, the less speed" (John Heywood). "Be fast, but don't hurry" (John Wooden).

A young and successful executive was traveling down a neighborhood street and going a bit too fast in his new Jaguar. He was watching for kids darting out from between parked cars and slowed down when he thought he saw something.

As his car passed, no children appeared. Instead, a brick smashed into the Jag's side door! He slammed on the brakes and drove the Jag back to the spot where the brick had been thrown. The angry driver then jumped out of the car, grabbed the nearest kid, and pushed him up against a parked car, shouting, "What was that all about and who are you? Just what the heck are you doing? That's a new car and that brick you threw is going to cost a lot of money. Why did you do it?"

The young boy was apologetic. "Please mister . . . please, I'm sorry . . . I didn't know what else to do," he pleaded. "I threw the brick because no one else would stop . . ."

With tears dripping down his face and off his chin, the youth pointed to a spot just around a parked car. "It's my brother," he said. "He rolled off the curb and fell out of his wheelchair and I can't lift him up."

Now sobbing, the boy asked the stunned executive, "Would you please help me get him back into his wheelchair? He's hurt and he's too heavy for me."

Moved beyond words, the driver tried to swallow the rapidly swelling lump in his throat. He hurriedly lifted the handicapped boy back into the wheelchair, then took out his fancy handkerchief and dabbed at the fresh scrapes and cuts. A quick look told him everything was going to be okay.

"Thank you, and may God bless you," the grateful child told the stranger. Too shook up for words, the man simply watched the little boy push his wheelchair-bound brother down the sidewalk toward their home.

It was a long, slow walk back to the Jaguar. The damage was very noticeable, but the driver never bothered to repair the dented side door. He kept the dent there to remind him of this message: don't go through life so fast that someone has to throw a brick at you to get your attention!

God whispers in our souls and speaks to our hearts. Sometimes when we don't have time to listen, He has to throw a brick at us. It's our choice: we can listen to the whisper . . . or wait for the brick!

It's more important to know where you're going than to see how fast you can get there. "Impatient people always get there too late" (Jean Dutourd). We undo ourselves by impatience.

One of the most frequent causes for failure among able-bodied people is impatience in waiting for results. "The haste of a fool is the slowest thing in the world" (Thomas Shadwell). Being in a hurry shows that the thing you are doing is too big for you. Impatience is one big "get-ahead-ache."

"There is a time to let things happen and a time to make things happen" (Hugh Prather). That's what Ecclesiastes 3:1 means when it says, "To everything there is a season, and a time to every purpose under the heaven."

Life is lived in seasons, which means we're to do different things at different times. It's simple: do the *right* thing at the *right* time. A Chinese proverb says, "Never leave your field in spring or your house in winter." God never sends a winter without the joy of spring, the growth of summer, or the harvest of fall.

Be a good finisher and never claim a victory prematurely. The greatest assassin of dreams is haste, the desire to reach things before the right time.

NUGGET #18

Forty Momentum Makers

Over the years, I've heard many Christian leaders say how a word from the Lord can change your life. I understand they mostly mean a direction or an idea. But God, literally with one word, can ignite something inside each of us, creating a kind of divine momentum. Consider the power and impact each of these words has for your own life.

1. Choice
2. Commitment
3. Decision
4. Faith
5. Prayer
6. Action
7. Focus
8. Small steps
9. Listening
10. Creativity
11. Standing alone
12. Wisdom

13. Zeal
14. Purpose
15. Positioning
16. Talents
17. The Word of God
18. Right friends
19. Change
20. Forgiveness
21. Pure heart
22. Right spirit
23. Excellence
24. Thanksgiving
25. Love
26. Persistence
27. Giving
28. Priorities
29. Risk
30. Vision
31. Compassion
32. Obedience
33. Servanthood
34. Yieldedness
35. Joy
36. Honesty
37. Character
38. Dreams
39. Patience
40. "Yes, Lord!"

NUGGET
#19

Stay Out of Your Own Way

Here's the first rule of winning: don't defeat yourself. Your biggest enemy is you. When you find yourself getting in your own way, you're like a refrigerator—slowly gathering ice, which, if allowed to accumulate unchecked, will reduce its effectiveness to nothing. God wisely designed the human body so we could neither pat our own backs nor kick ourselves too easily.

The first and best victory is to conquer yourself. Dwight L. Moody said, "I have never met a man who has given me as much trouble as myself." All significant battles are waged within one's self. Don't build a case against yourself.

When you find yourself standing in your own way, you'll always hope vaguely and dread precisely. Talk back to your internal critic. "If you want to move your greatest obstacle, realize that your obstacle is yourself—and that the time to act is now" (Nido Qubein).

Very often a change of self is needed more than a change of scene. Only you can hold yourself back . . . only you can stand in your own way . . . only you can help yourself. There's no one to stop you but yourself.

I came across this list of five lessons from the pencil:

1. You will be able to do many great things, but only if you allow yourself to work hand in hand with others.
2. You will experience a painful sharpening from time to time, but you'll need it to become better.
3. You're equipped to correct any mistakes you might make.
4. The most important part of you will always be what's inside.
5. On every surface you are used on, you must leave your mark.

No matter what the condition, you must continue to write.

You must begin to think of yourself as becoming the person you want to be. "Give the man you'd like to be a look at the man you are" (Edgar Guest). Change what you tell yourself. The Bible tells us, "For God made Christ, who never sinned, to be the offering for our sin, so that we could be made right with God through Christ" (2 Cor. 5:21 NLT).

"No one really knows enough to be a pessimist" (Norman Cousins). Remember, "One of the nice things about problems is that a good many of them do not exist except in our imaginations" (Steve Allen). The fear you fear is only in yourself and nowhere else.

Two forces war within us. One says you can't. The other says that with God you can. "It's not the mountain we conquer, but ourselves" (Sir Edmund Hillary). The problem most people have is that they are the problem.

Part 2

LOOKING OUTWARD

NUGGET #20

Paths without Obstacles
Don't Lead Anywhere

To get to the Promised Land, you'll have to navigate your way through the wilderness. We all encounter obstacles, problems, and challenges that cross our path. How we respond to them is one of the most important decisions we make.

> Dear brothers, is your life full of difficulties and temptations? Then be happy, for when the way is rough, your patience has a chance to grow. So let it grow, and don't try to squirm out of your problems. For when your patience is finally in full bloom, then you'll be ready for anything, strong in character, full and complete. (James 1:2–4 TLB)

A person with twenty difficulties is twice as alive as a person with only ten. If you haven't got any challenges, you should get down on your knees and ask, "Lord, don't you trust me anymore?" So what if you've got problems? That's good! Why? Consistent victories over your problems are like steps on your stairway to success. Be thankful for your obstacles; if they were less difficult, someone with less ability would have your job.

"A successful man will never see the day that does not bring a fresh quota of problems, and the mark of success is to deal with them effectively" (Lauris Norstad). James Bilkey observed, "You will never be the person you can be if pressure, tension and discipline are taken out of your life." Refuse to let yourself become discouraged by temporary setbacks. If you are beginning to encounter some hard bumps, don't worry. At least you're out of a rut. Circumstances are not your master.

Two women were talking, and one asked the other how many times she'd been married. "Four," was the reply.

"Four times!" exclaimed the first woman. "Why so many?"

So the other woman explained: "Well, I first got married when I was very young, and I married this wonderful man who was a banker. However, one day just a few weeks after we were married, his bank was robbed and he was shot and killed."

"Oh my gosh, that's terrible!" the first woman said.

"Well, it wasn't that tragic. Soon after that, I started seeing another man who performed in the circus. He was really a great guy, but he lived pretty dangerously because he performed his high-wire act without a net. Well, a few weeks after we got married, he was performing a show and suddenly a gust of wind came by and knocked him off his wire and he was killed."

"Your second husband was killed too? That's horrible!"

"Yes, it was terrible, but at the funeral I fell in love with the minister and we got married soon after that. Unfortunately, one Sunday while he was walking to church, he was hit by a car and killed."

"Three? Three husbands of yours were killed? How could you live through all that?"

"It was pretty tough, but then I met my present husband. And he's a wonderful man. I think we'll live a long, happy life together."

"And what does your present husband do for a living?"

"He's a mortician."

"A mortician? I don't understand something here. First you marry a banker, then a circus performer, then a minister, and now a mortician? Why such a diverse group of husbands?"

"Well, if you think about it, it's not too hard to understand. One for the money . . . two for the show . . . three to get ready . . . and four to go!"

You can always tell a lot about a person by the number of challenges it takes to discourage them. When the water starts to rise, *you can too*! You can go over, not under. "Obstacles across our path can be spiritual flat tires—disruptions in our lives seem to be disastrous at the time, but end by redirecting our lives in a meaningful way" (Bernie Siegel).

The truth is, if you find a path with no obstacles, it's probably a path that doesn't lead to anywhere important. Adversity is the mother of invention. And our adversity is always God's opportunity. Adversity gives birth to opportunity. "In this world you will have trouble. But take heart! I have overcome the world" (John 16:33 NIV).

"What is the difference between an obstacle and an opportunity? Our attitude towards it. Every opportunity has a difficulty, and every difficulty has an opportunity" (J. Sidlow Baxter). "Show me someone who has done something worthwhile, and I'll show you someone who has overcome adversity" (Lou Holtz). Many people have good intentions, but then something bad happens and they simply stop. Every path has a puddle, but those puddles can be God telling us where to step.

The travel is worth the travail when you're on the right road. Just recognize that life is challenging . . . then things will be much easier for you.

> Every problem has in it the seeds of its own solution. If you don't have any problems, you don't get any seeds.
>
> Norman Vincent Peale

Watch out for emergencies. They are your big chance! Live your life so you can say, "I've had a life full of challenges, thank God!"

NUGGET
#21

Don't Measure Yourself with Another's Coat

A heart surgeon took his car to the local garage for a regular service. While he waited, he usually exchanged a little friendly banter with the owner, a skilled but not especially wealthy mechanic.

"So tell me," said the mechanic, "I've been wondering about what we both do for a living, and how much more you get paid than me."

"Yes?" said the surgeon.

"Well, look at this," said the mechanic, as he worked on a big, complicated engine. "I check how it's running, open it up, fix the valves, and put it all back together so it works good as new. We basically do the same job, don't we? And yet you are paid ten times what I am—how do you explain that?"

The surgeon thought for a moment, then smiling gently he replied, "Try it with the engine running."

"Every man must do two things alone. He must do his own believing and his own dying" (Martin Luther). When you compare yourself with others, you'll become either bitter or vain. There are always greater and lesser persons than you. Making comparisons is a sure path to frustration, but *comparison is never proof.* "You can't clear your own fields while counting the rocks on your neighbor's farm" (Joan Welch). "The grass may be greener on the other side of the fence, but there's probably more of it to mow" (Lois Cory). Hills look small and green a long way off.

You waste your energy, time, and effort when you compare yourself to others. What happens in another person's life has no impact and no effect on what happens in yours.

I was dismayed when I heard from a friend I hadn't seen for three or four years. He told me he felt bad in *his* life because of some of the success that had happened in *mine.* I couldn't help being perplexed at his comments, and I responded to him by saying, "Do you mean you would have felt a lot better if I'd done horribly the last three or four years?" Well, of course he said no. It just points out the fact that what's happening in another person's life is not a basis for how good or how bad you're doing in your own. Success in someone else's life doesn't hurt the chances for success in yours.

Life is more fun when you don't keep score for others. When you compare your place and plan with others, they're never accurate. *Nothing is as it appears!*

Success is simply a matter of doing what you do best and not worrying about what the other person is going to do. You carry success or failure within yourself; it doesn't depend on outside conditions.

Ask yourself the question Earl Nightingale once posed: "Are you motivated by what you really want out of life, or are you mass-motivated?" Make sure you decide what you really want, not what someone else wants for you. Do you say, "I'm good, but not as good as I ought to be"? Or do you say, "I'm not as bad as a lot of other people"? The longer you dwell on another's weakness, the more you affect your own mind with unhappiness. You must create your own system, your own plan, or you'll be enslaved by another person's. Don't reason and compare. Your purpose is to create, not re-create.

"We only become what we are by the radical and deep-seated refusal of that which others have made of us" (Jean-Paul Sartre). Every person who trims himself to suit everybody else will soon find himself whittled away. So don't measure your situation against that of others. Measure your situation against God's will and His Word for your life.

If a thousand people say a foolish thing, it is still a foolish thing. Direction from God is never a matter of consensus or public opinion. A wise man makes his own decision; an ignorant man follows public opinion. Don't think you're necessarily on the right road just because it's a well-beaten path. The greatest risk in life is to wait for and depend on others for your security. Don't measure yourself with another man's coat. Don't judge yourself through someone else's eyes.

NUGGET #22

Invest in Others

One of the most exciting decisions you can make is to be on the lookout for opportunities to invest in others. For me, this has been one of the most powerful principles of momentum I've implemented in my life.

I remember driving with my family from St. Louis to Tulsa, Oklahoma. I was listening to a Zig Ziglar audio book. He said, "You'll always have everything you want in life if you'll help enough others get what they want." When I heard this statement, something literally went off inside of me and I said out loud, "I'm going to do it. I'm going to aggressively help as many people as I can to get what they want out of life." That decision to look for ways to help others, to invest in them, changed my life and continues today.

One of the marks of true greatness is to develop greatness in others. "There are three keys to more abundant living: caring about others, daring for others, and sharing with others" (William Ward). I've found that really great leaders have a unique perspective. They understand that greatness is not deposited in them to stay but rather to flow through them into others. "We make a living by what we get, but we make a life by what we give" (Norman MacEwan). Assign yourself the purpose of making others happy and thereby give yourself a gift.

People have a way of becoming what you encourage them to be. Be sincerely interested in helping others. Ralph Waldo Emerson observed, "Trust men and they will be true to you; treat them greatly and they will show themselves great." Spend your life lifting people up, not putting people down. "Treat people as if they were what they ought to be and you help them to become what they are capable of being" (Goethe).

Whatever we praise, we increase. There's no investment you can make that will pay you so well as the effort to scatter sunshine and good cheer into others throughout your life journey.

> The person who renders loyal service in a humble capacity will be chosen for higher responsibilities, just as the biblical servant who multiplied the one pound given by his master was made ruler over ten cities.
>
> B. C. Forbes

There are two types of people in the world: those who come into a room and say, "Here I am!" and those who come in and say, "Ah, there you are!" How do you know a good person? A good person makes others good. Find happiness by helping others find it.

The story goes that over two hundred years ago, a man dressed in civilian clothes rode past a field where a small group of exhausted, battle-weary soldiers were digging an obviously important defensive position. Their section leader, himself making no effort to help, was shouting orders, threatening punishment if the work was not completed within the hour.

"Why are you not helping?" asked the stranger on horseback.

"I am in charge. The men do as I tell them," said the section leader. Then he added, "Help them yourself if you feel strongly about it."

To the section leader's surprise, the stranger dismounted and helped the men until the job was finished.

Before leaving, the stranger congratulated the men for their work and approached the puzzled section leader.

"You should notify top command next time your rank prevents you from supporting your men—and I will provide a more permanent solution," said the stranger.

Up close, the section leader now recognized General George Washington—and also the lesson he'd just been taught.

"What you make happen for others, God will make happen for you" (Mike Murdock). "Knowing that whatsoever good thing any man doeth, the same shall he receive of the Lord" (Eph. 6:8). A good deed bears interest. You cannot hold a light to another's path without brightening your own. Develop greatness in others.

There is no more noble occupation in the world than to assist another human being—to help someone succeed.

Allan McGinnis

The true meaning of life is to plant trees under whose shade you do not expect to sit.

Nelson Henderson

The greatest use of your life is to spend it for something and on someone who will outlast it. "If you cannot win, make the one ahead of you break the record" (Jan McKeithen). Invest in others. It pays great dividends.

NUGGET
#23

You Don't Learn Anything While You're Talking

One of the best ways to persuade others is by listening to them. You'll find a gossip talks to you about others, a bore talks to you about himself, and a brilliant conversationalist talks to you about yourself and listens to what you say. You don't learn anything while you're talking. The truth is, the more you say the less people remember. When it comes to listening, it's always more blessed to receive than to give.

"Keep your mouth closed and you'll stay out of trouble" (Prov. 21:23 TLB). A person is known by the silence he or she keeps. Don't miss many valuable opportunities to hold your tongue and listen to what the other person is saying.

When you have nothing to say, say nothing. Silence is a friend who will never betray you.

The greatest skill you can develop is the skill of listening to others. Say as little as possible to get the point across.

The obituary department of a local newspaper received a phone call one day. The caller asked, "How much do funeral notices cost?"

"Five dollars per word, ma'am," came the operator's response.

"Good. Do you have a paper and pencil handy?"

"Yes, ma'am."

"Okay, write this: 'Fred dead.'"

"I'm sorry, ma'am; I forgot to tell you there's a five-word minimum."

"Humph," came the reply. "You certainly did forget to tell me that."

A moment of silence.

"Got your pencil and paper?"

"Yes, ma'am."

"Okay, print this: 'Fred dead, Cadillac for sale.'"

The man of few words and settled mind is wise; therefore, even a fool is thought to be wise when he is silent. It pays him to keep his mouth shut. (Prov. 17:27–28 TLB)

Talk is cheap because supply exceeds demand. "As you go through life, you're going to have many opportunities to keep your mouth shut. Take advantage of all of them" (*West Virginia Gazette*). There must have been some reason God made human ears to stay open and human mouths to shut. As one grows older and wiser, one talks less and says more.

Learn to listen. Sometimes opportunity disguises itself this way and knocks very softly. You will find that God speaks for those who hold their peace. Silence can be golden.

Too much talk always includes error. There is only one rule for being a good talker: be a good listener. Your ears will never get you into trouble. One of the most powerful principles you can implement in your life is the principle of listening to others. "Don't talk so much. You keep putting your foot in your mouth. Be sensible and turn off the flow!" (Prov. 10:19 TLB).

NUGGET
#24

Don't Let Things Stick to You

As I've had the privilege of meeting hundreds of people over the past several years, one thing that always stood out to me is how many people have things attached to them. People allow a critical statement made by a third-grade teacher, a failure or mistake they made ten or fifteen years ago, or the comments a noisy, negative neighbor made last week to hold them back from their destiny.

Only a foolish person adheres to all she hears. *Not everyone has a right to speak into your life.* This is one of the most powerful principles you can apply to acquire momentum.

I really believe one of the major benefits of asking forgiveness from God is that things no longer "stick" to us. He says that if we confess our sins, He is faithful and just to forgive us of our sins. That would be great enough, but incredibly God doesn't stop there. He also promises to cleanse us from all unrighteousness (see 1 John 1:9). When He cleanses us, we have a right standing before the Father. Why? He doesn't want things to stick to us. Because of our right standing before the Father, we're now free of the failures and mistakes, the wrong words and attitudes of the past, and we are released to accomplish things for the future.

I've found that successful people have a way of not letting things stick to them.

One Sunday morning before the services began, people were sitting in their pews and talking about their lives, their families, and so forth. Suddenly the devil appeared at the front of the church. Everyone started screaming and running for the exit, trampling one another in a frantic effort to get away from him.

Soon everyone was evacuated from the church except for one elderly gentleman who sat calmly in his pew, not moving . . . seemingly oblivious to the fact that God's ultimate enemy was in his presence.

Now this confused Satan a bit, so he walked up to the man and said, "Don't you know who I am?"

The man replied, "Yep, sure do."

Satan asked, "Aren't you afraid of me?"

"Nope, sure ain't," said the man.

Satan was a little perturbed at this and queried, "Why aren't you afraid of me?"

The man calmly replied, "Been married to your sister for over forty-eight years."

Like this elderly man, don't let stuff stick to you.

Don't worry if you don't get what you think you should. What seems so necessary today might not even be desirable tomorrow. "In times like these, it helps to recall that there have always been times like these" (Paul Harvey). If we could forget our troubles as easily as we forget our blessings, how different things would be.

One way to be free of things that want to stick to you is to take your mind off the things that seem to be against you. Thinking about these negative factors builds into them a power they don't truly possess. Talking about your grievances merely adds to those grievances.

Attach yourself to God's forgiveness, to His plan, and to His Word. Then watch yourself become loosed from former "sticky" situations.

**NUGGET
#25**

Be the First to Forgive

Living a life of unforgiveness is like driving your car with your parking brake on. It causes you to slow down and lose your momentum. And you end up being worn-out!

One of the most expensive luxuries you can possess is to be unforgiving toward someone. A deep-seated grudge in your life eats away at your peace of mind like a deadly cancer, destroying a vital organ of life. In fact, there are few things as pathetic and terrible to behold as a person who has harbored a grudge for many years.

The heaviest load you can possibly carry is a pack of grudges. So if you want to travel far and fast, then travel light. Unpack all of your envy, jealousy, unforgiveness, revenge, and fear.

Never reject forgiveness or the opportunity to forgive. The weak can never forgive because forgiveness is a characteristic of the strong. When you live a life of unforgiveness, revenge naturally follows. But revenge is the deceiver. It looks sweet, but it's most often bitter. It always costs more to revenge a wrong than to bear it. You can't win by trying to even the score.

Be the first to forgive. Forgiveness can be your deepest need and highest achievement. Many times it's the first step of an answer to prayer or release of a miracle. Without forgiveness, life is governed by an endless cycle of resentment and retaliation. What a dreadful waste of effort. "He who has not forgiven an enemy has never yet tasted one of the most sublime enjoyments of life," declares Johann Lavater.

Forgiving those who have wronged you is a key to your personal peace. What the world needs is peace that passes all *mis*understanding. Forgiveness also releases you for action and freedom.

"Never cut what can be untied" (Joseph Jobert). Don't burn bridges. You'll be surprised how many times you have to cross over that same river. Unforgiveness is empty, but forgiveness makes a future possible. You'll "get out of the right side of the bed" and "start your day on the right foot" if you ask yourself every day, "Whom do I need to forgive?"

NUGGET #26

There Are Million-Dollar Ideas around You Every Day

Sometimes as I drive in different parts of the city where I live, I can't help but notice the vast variety of businesses. Many times I pause and think, "That's someone's dream, that's someone's unique idea, that's someone's million-dollar opportunity." I believe there are significant opportunities and ideas around you every day. In fact, "God hides things by putting them near us" (Ralph Waldo Emerson).

The best opportunities and ideas are hidden near you. The Bible says, "The earth is full of the goodness of the LORD" (Ps. 33:5). You can see a thousand miracles around you every day . . . or nothing. Oral Roberts put it this way: "Miracles are coming to you or by you, every day." Your big opportunity may be right where you are now.

There are no limits to your possibilities. At any moment, you have more possibilities than you can act upon. Too many people spend their whole lives only solving problems and not recognizing opportunities. Change how you view life and you'll discover what you thought wasn't there.

> Chocolate is derived from cocoa beans. A bean is a vegetable. Sugar is derived from either sugar CANE or sugar BEETS. Both are plants, which places them in the vegetable category. Thus, chocolate is a vegetable.
>
> Now, eat your vegetables!

Where do you hear opportunity knocking? How can you answer that knock? "There are always opportunities everywhere, just as there always have been" (Charles Fillmore). Earl Nightingale said, "You are, at this moment, standing right in the middle of your own 'acres of diamonds.'" He also pointed out, "Wherever there is danger, there lurks opportunity; wherever there is opportunity, there lurks danger. The two are inseparable. They go together."

A successful person "always has a number of projects planned, to which he looks forward. Any one of them could change the course of his life overnight" (Mark Caine). Opportunities? They're all around us . . . lying dormant everywhere, waiting for the observant eye to discover them. Look at the same thing as everyone else but see something different. "Eye hath not seen, nor ear heard, neither have entered into the heart of man, the things which God hath prepared for them that love him" (1 Cor. 2:9).

There's a legendary story illustrating the difference between positive thinking and negative thinking:

> Many years ago two salesmen were sent by a British shoe manufacturer to Africa to investigate and report back on market potential. The first salesman reported back, "There is no potential here—nobody wears shoes."
>
> The second salesman reported back, "There is massive potential here—nobody wears shoes."

This simple story provides one of the best examples of how a single situation may be viewed in two quite different ways—negatively or positively.

We could also explain this in terms of seeing a situation's problems and disadvantages instead of its opportunities and benefits.

The stars are constantly shining, but we often do not see them until dark hours. The same is true with opportunities. It's true what the cartoon character Pogo said: "Gentlemen, we're surrounded by insurmountable opportunities."

NUGGET #27

Forty Momentum Breakers

Let's face it, it's easy to start a two-mile run, begin a new diet, or initiate writing a book. The big question is, can you finish? Every endeavor, great or small, presents obstacles along the way, tempting us to quit. Some of these are outside of our control, but most we bring on ourselves. I call them momentum breakers. Momentum is simply moving forward in the right direction. The key is overcoming some of these "breakers" along the way.

1. Indecision
2. Complaining
3. Fear
4. Worry
5. Regret
6. Overreaction
7. The past
8. Greed

9. Excuses
10. Tradition
11. Envy
12. Criticism
13. Wrong friends
14. Mistakes
15. Unforgiveness
16. Procrastination
17. Distractions
18. Lying
19. Quitting
20. Double-mindedness
21. Hesitation
22. Talking
23. Failures
24. Delay
25. Jealousy
26. Impatience
27. Aimlessness
28. Disobedience
29. Strife
30. Misdirection
31. Conformity
32. Dishonesty
33. Ingratitude
34. Security
35. Lukewarmness
36. Hate
37. Anger
38. Lust
39. Laziness
40. "No, Lord."

NUGGET
#28

There Are Good Ships and Bad Ships, but the Best Ships Are Friendships

Who you choose to be your closest friends or associates is one of the most important decisions you make during the course of your life. "You are the same today that you are going to be five years from now except for two things: the people with whom you associate and the books you read" (Charlie "Tremendous" Jones). The Bible says if you associate with wise men you'll become wise, but a companion of fools will be destroyed (see Prov. 13:20). You do become like those with whom you closely associate.

"Friends in your life are like pillars on your porch. Sometimes they hold you up, sometimes they lean on you, and sometimes it's just enough to know they're standing by" (Anonymous). "Iron sharpeneth iron; so a man sharpeneth the countenance of his friend" (Prov. 27:17). A real friend is a person who, when you've made a fool of yourself, let's you forget it. Good friendship always multiplies your joy and divides your grief.

I've found that the best friends are those who bring out the best in you, and a real good friend is someone who knows all about you and likes you anyway. A true friend is someone who is there for you when they'd rather be somewhere else. "A friend loveth at all times, and a brother is born for adversity" (Prov. 17:17). I believe we should keep our friendships in constant repair. In addition to loving our enemies, we should remember to treat our friends well too.

The wrong kind of friends, unlike the good kind of friends, brings out the worst, not the best, in you. You know the kind I'm talking about. They're the people who absorb sunshine and radiate gloom. The fact is not everyone will want you to succeed, no matter how hard you try.

An elderly man lay dying in his bed. In death's agony, he suddenly smelled the aroma of his favorite chocolate chip cookies wafting up the stairs. He gathered his remaining strength and lifted himself from his bed. Leaning against the wall, he slowly made his way out of his bedroom, and with even greater effort forced himself down the stairs, gripping the railing with both hands. With labored breath, he leaned against the doorframe while gazing into the kitchen.

Were it not for death's agony, he would have thought himself already in heaven. There, spread out on newspapers on the kitchen table, were literally hundreds of his favorite chocolate chip cookies. Was it heaven? Or was it one final act of heroic love from his devoted wife, seeing to it that he left this world a happy man?

Mustering one great final effort, he threw himself toward the table, landing on his knees in a rumpled posture. His parched lips parted; the wondrous taste of the cookie was already in his mouth, seemingly bringing him back to life. His aged, withered, shaking hand made its way to a cookie at the edge of the table, when his wife suddenly smacked it with a spatula. "Stay out of those," she said. "They're for the funeral."

There are people who will always come up with reasons why you can't do what you know you're supposed to do. *Ignore them!* The Bible says in Proverbs 25:19, "Putting confidence in an unreliable man is like chewing with a sore tooth, or trying to run on a broken foot" (TLB).

A day away from the wrong associations is like a month in the country. "Keep away from people who try to belittle your ambitions. Small people always do that, but the really great make you feel that you, too, can become great" (Mark Twain). Never have a companion who casts you in the shade.

True friends don't sympathize with your weakness—they help summon your strength. "Treat your friends as you do your best pictures, and place them in their best light" (Jennie Churchill). Friends communicate at the heart level. There are good ships and there are bad ships, but the best ships are friendships.

A good friend never gets in your way . . . unless you're on your way down. A good friend is one who walks in when others walk out. The right kind of friends are those with whom you can dare to be yourself and with whom you can dream out loud. For me, my best friends are those who understand my past, believe in my future, and accept me today just the way I am.

NUGGET
#29

Dig for Diamonds, Don't Chase Butterflies

Pay more attention to the things that are working positively in your life than to those that are giving you trouble. Too many times people devote the majority of their effort, time, and attention to those things in their lives that are never going to be productive. "If a man could have half his wishes, he would double his troubles" (Ben Franklin).

One of the devil's primary strategies to hinder our momentum is using distractions to keep us from being focused on the plan God has for us. Determine what you really want and what God wants for you. This will keep you from chasing butterflies and put you to work digging for diamonds.

Clear your mind of what's out of your control so you can focus on and act upon your goals for the day. You'll always get lost by trying to find an alternate route for the straight and narrow. "He will keep in perfect peace all those who trust in him, whose thoughts turn often to the Lord!" (Isa. 26:3 TLB). "Life's greatest tragedy is to lose God and not miss Him" (F. W. Norwood).

The words of others will be one of the primary distractions through which Satan will try to hinder you. Just once do what others say you can't do and you'll never pay attention to their limitations again. If you let other people stop you, they will.

When you allow yourself to be distracted by the fear and doubt others want to bring into your life, you'll have a quick ear for bad news, large eyes for trouble ahead, and be a great inventor of things that will never happen. Jesus said, "Anyone who lets himself be distracted from the work I plan for him is not fit for the Kingdom of God" (Luke 9:62 TLB).

Concentrate on one thing at a time and rule out any outside influences that have no real bearing on the task at hand. By doing that, you'll bring all of your mind and faculties without distraction to the problem or subject at hand.

> People are always blaming their circumstances for what they are. I don't believe in circumstances. The people who get on in this world are the people who get up and look for circumstances they want, and, if they can't find them, make them.
>
> George Bernard Shaw

Within your concentration the rest of the world cannot distract you. "Look straight ahead; don't even turn your head to look. Watch your step. Stick to the path and be safe" (Prov. 4:25–26 TLB).

NUGGET
#30

Nothing Great
Is Created Suddenly

One of the most common prayers I pray for others (and for myself) is this: "Lord, please send small opportunities across their paths to do what You've called them to do." When we're faithful in those small opportunities, God says, "You have been faithful in handling this small amount . . . so now I will give you many more responsibilities. Begin the joyous tasks I have assigned to you" (Matt. 25:21 TLB).

People who think they're too big to do little things are perhaps too little to be asked to do big things. Small opportunities are often the beginning of great enterprises.

Nothing great is created suddenly. Nothing can be done except little by little. Never decide to do nothing just because you can only do a little. Within that little thing lies a big opportunity. Small things make a big difference; therefore, do all it takes to be successful in little things.

You'll never do great things if you can't do small things in a great way. All difficult things have their beginning in that which is easy, and all great things in that which is small. One of the major factors that sets apart people who have momentum from those who don't is that they pay attention to small ideas and opportunities.

The courage to begin is the same courage it takes to succeed. The courage to begin separates dreamers from achievers. The beginning is the most important part of any endeavor. Even worse than a quitter is the person who's afraid to begin. "Winning starts with beginning" (Robert Schuller).

Ninety percent of success is showing up and starting. You may be disappointed if you fail, but you're doomed if you don't try. Don't be deceived: knowledge of a path can never be a substitute for diligently putting one foot in front of the other.

Discover step-by-step excitement. The first step is the hardest. "That's why many fail—because they don't get started—they don't go. They don't overcome inertia. They don't begin" (W. Clement Stone).

Dare to begin. No endeavor is worse than that which is not attempted. You don't know what you can do until you have tried. People, like trees, must grow or wither. There's no standing still. Do what you can. The next move is yours!

NUGGET
#31

No Person Is More Cheated
Than the Selfish Man

The way to grow is to give. Here's a simple but powerful principle: *give people more than they expect and do it cheerfully.* "And whosoever shall compel thee to go a mile, go with him twain" (Matt. 5:41). "If there be any truer measure of a man than by what he does, it must be by what he gives" (Robert South).

It's a universal law—we have to give before we get. In giving to others you'll find yourself blessed. The giver's harvest is always full. To get, give. Getters don't get—givers get. When you give yourself, you'll receive more than you give.

We tire of the pleasures we take but never of those we give. The person who sows seeds of kindness will have a perpetual harvest. Be kinder than necessary. Kindness is a hard thing to give away . . . it keeps coming back to the giver. Proverbs 11:17 says, "Your own soul is nourished when you are kind; it is destroyed when you are cruel" (TLB).

One great way to give is in words of appreciation. A complement is like verbal sunshine. "How forcible are right words!" (Job 6:25). So never be sparing with words of appreciation, especially when those around you deserve them. Everyone loves praise. Look hard for ways to give it to them. The good words you give are worth much and cost so little.

That which you can't give away, you don't possess . . . it possesses you. "A man's life consisteth not in the abundance of the things which he possesseth" (Luke 12:15). Remember, what you give will bring you more pleasure than what you get. If you are selfish, you'll find yourself bounded on the north, south, east, and west by just yourself. No man is more cheated than the selfish man.

God is a giver. So be like Him and do good to everyone. Be quick to give because when you give right away, it's like giving twice. Giving can become a *good* habit.

"The man who will use his skill and constructive imagination to see how much he can give for a dollar instead of how little he can give for a dollar is bound to succeed" (Henry Ford). We must not only give what we have; we must also give what we are. "You can give without loving, but you cannot love without giving" (Amy Carmichael). Love's first response is to give.

NUGGET
#32

Pick a Problem Bigger Than You

People nearly always pick a problem their own size and ignore or leave to others the bigger or smaller ones. Pick a problem bigger than you. "Success—real success—in any endeavor demands more from an individual than most people are willing to offer—not more than they are capable of offering" (James Roche). If you've achieved all you've planned for yourself, you've not planned enough.

The desire for safety stands against every great and virtuous dream. Security is the first step toward stagnation. The trouble with this world is that too many people try to go through life with a catcher's mitt on both hands.

Boldness in vision is the first, second, and third most important thing. He who dares nothing should expect nothing. "One who is contented with what he has done will never be famous for what he will do" (Christian Bovee).

Be used for a mighty purpose. Martin Luther King Jr. said, "A man who won't die for something is not fit to live." Dare to do what's right for you. Choose a goal for which you are willing to exchange a piece of your life. The surest way to happiness is to lose yourself in a cause greater than you. You'll be unhappy if you don't reach for something beyond yourself.

"It is difficult to say what is impossible, for the dream of yesterday is the hope of today and the reality of tomorrow" (Robert Goddard). Reality is something you can rise above. Every great action is impossible when it is undertaken. Only after it has become accomplished does it seem possible to the average man. To small thinkers everything looks like a mountain. The grandest things are, in some ways, the easiest to do because there is so little competition.

To be complacently satisfied with yourself is a sure sign progress is about to end. If you're satisfied with yourself, you'd better change your ideals. "How much better to know that we have dared to live our dreams than to live our lives in a lethargy of regret" (Gilbert Caplin).

Moderation is a fatal thing. Nothing succeeds like excess.

Oscar Wilde

You'll never succeed beyond your wildest dreams . . . unless you have some wild dreams.

NUGGET
#33

What Works? Work on That

Everyone who got where they are had to begin where they were. Only one person in a thousand knows how to really live in the present. The problem is we seldom think of what we have, but we always think of what we lack.

Failures wish they could do things they *can't* do. They think little of what they *can* do. What you *can* do . . . you can *do*.

"We don't need more strength or more ability or greater opportunity. What we need to use is what we have" (Basil Walsh). People are always ignoring something they can do and trying to do something they can't. Learning new things won't help you if you aren't using what you already know. Success means doing the best you can with what you have.

"We've all heard we have to learn from our mistakes, but I think it is more important to learn from our successes. If you learn only from your mistakes, you are inclined to learn only errors" (Norman Vincent Peale). Some people spend their whole lives failing and never even notice.

The person who gets ahead is the one who does more than is necessary—and keeps on doing it. No matter how rough the path, some forge ahead; no matter how easy the going, some lag behind. Begin somewhere—you cannot build your reputation on what you intend to do. The only way to be gone is to not stay here.

The main thing wrong with doing nothing is that you never know when you are finished. When you are through improving, you're through. Use whatever you have been given and more will come to you. Never leave well enough alone. "Opportunities multiply as they are seized; they die when neglected" (Anonymous). Every ceiling, when reached, becomes a floor upon which one walks and now can see a new ceiling. "Every exit is an entry somewhere" (Tom Stoppard).

> You can't control the weather, but you can control the moral atmosphere that surrounds you. Why worry about things you can't control? Get busy controlling the things that depend upon you.
>
> *In a Nutshell*

> A strong, successful man is not the victim of his environment. He creates favorable conditions.
>
> Orison Marden

The best way to better your lot is to do a lot better. Build on the lot in life you've been given.

NUGGET
#34

Don't Belittle . . . Be Big

People with momentum have a common trait—they attract criticism. How you respond to criticism will determine the rate of your momentum. The person who never steps on anybody's toes is probably standing still. I was reading a cover story on Billy Graham in *Time* magazine recently and was surprised to find several sharp criticisms of him from *fellow ministers*. I was reminded that all great men face great criticism. Sticks and stones are thrown only at fruit-bearing trees.

Learn to expect unjust criticisms for your goals and accomplishments. Even Jesus (who was perfect) was repeatedly criticized. If Jesus was criticized, then surely Billy Graham, you, and I will be also.

It can be beneficial to receive constructive criticism from those who have your best interests at heart and are of like mind, but you're not responsible to respond to those who don't. You're responsible to respond to God. "Throw out the mocker, and you will be rid of tension, fighting, and quarrels" (Prov. 22:10 TLB). Don't replace time spent with a friend by giving it to a critic. I like what Edward Gibbon said: "I never make the mistake of arguing with people for whose opinions I have no respect."

It's a thousand times easier to criticize than to create. That's why critics are never problem solvers. "Any fool can criticize, condemn and complain, and most do" (Dale Carnegie). My belief is that the person who says it cannot be done should not interrupt the one who is doing it. Just remember, when you're kicked from behind, it must mean you're out in front. A Yiddish proverb says, "A critic is like the girl who can't dance, so she says the band can't play."

Critics know the answers without having probed deep enough to know the questions. When threatened by miraculous truth, they respond with the "facts." "Don't let others spoil your faith and joy with their philosophies, their wrong and shallow answers built on men's thoughts and ideas, instead of on what Christ has said" (Col. 2:8 TLB).

"A critic is a man created to praise greater men than himself, but he is never able to find them" (Richard LeGallienne). Critics are convinced that the chief purpose of sunshine is to cast shadows. They don't believe in anything, but they still want you to believe in them. A critic always knows the "price of everything and the value of nothing" (Oscar Wilde). Don't waste time responding to your critics, because you owe nothing to a critic.

Don't belittle—be big. Don't become a critic. "We have no more right to put our discordant states of mind into the lives of those around us and rob them of their sunshine and brightness than we have to enter their houses and steal their silverware" (Julia Seton). Remember, in criticizing others, you'll work overtime for no pay. "Wherein thou judgest another, thou condemnest thyself" (Rom. 2:1).

Never throw mud: you may hit your mark, but you will have dirty hands. Don't be a cloud because you failed to become a star. "Give so much time to the improvement of yourself that you have no time to criticize others" (Optimist Creed). Spend your time and energy creating, not criticizing.

> A good thing to remember,
> A better thing to do—
> Work with the construction gang,
> Not the wrecking crew.
>
> Anonymous

NUGGET #35

Envy Never Enriched Anyone

Picture a runner in full stride. He speeds through a pack of contenders, but he begins to look around at the competition. What is the inevitable conclusion to this scene? That runner will certainly slow down and will probably stumble. The same thing happens to us if we allow the distraction of envy to turn our heads as we run the race God has set before us. Instead of breaking records we're now breaking momentum. Envy weighs us down.

On Lake Isabella, located in the high desert an hour east of Bakersfield, California, some folks who were new to boating were having a problem. No matter how hard they tried, they couldn't get their brand-new, twenty-two-foot Bayliner to perform. It wouldn't stay level and was sluggish in almost every maneuver, no matter how much power was applied.

After about an hour of trying to make it go, they putted to a nearby marina, thinking someone there could tell them what was wrong. A thorough topside check revealed that everything was in perfect working condition.

The engine ran fine, the outdrive went up and down, the prop was the correct size and pitch. So one of the marina guys jumped in the water to check underneath. He came up choking on water, he was laughing so hard.

Under the boat, still strapped securely in place, was the trailer.

Like the trailer in this story, envy affects everything. It distorts and weighs down our progress. "Envy shoots at others and wounds herself" (English proverb). It's literally self-punishment.

"The man who covets is always poor" (Claudian). Envy never enriched any man. "Of all the passions, jealousy is that which exacts the hardest service and pays the bitterest wages. Its service is to watch the success of our enemy; its wages, to be sure of it" (Charles Colton).

Envy is like biting a dog because the dog bit you. "A relaxed attitude lengthens a man's life; jealousy rots it away" (Prov. 14:30 TLB). Like rust consumes iron, envy consumes a person. It drains the joy, satisfaction, and purpose out of living.

If allowed to grow, envy breeds hatred and revenge. To be angry and to seek revenge is like praying to the devil. The Bible says, "Also, see that no one pays back evil for evil, but always try to do good to each other and to everyone else" (1 Thess. 5:15 TLB). Revenge converts a little right into a big wrong.

"It is not love that's blind, but jealousy" (Lawrence Durrell). Envy sees the sea but not the rocks.

When an envious man hears another praised, he feels himself injured.

English proverb

Love looks through a telescope, envy through a microscope.

Josh Billings

Beware of covetousness: for a man's life consisteth not in the abundance of things which he possesseth. (Luke 12:15)

A wise person doesn't long for the things they don't have but rejoices in those things they do have. Continually compare what you want with what you have and you'll be unhappy. Instead, compare what you deserve with what you have and you'll be happy. Decide to stick with love. Envy is too great a burden to bear.

Part 3

LOOKING UPWARD

NUGGET
#36

Count God's Blessings, Don't Discount Them

Be aggressively thankful. When it comes to living your life, an important issue is whether you take things for granted or take them with gratitude. Thanksgiving is an attitude of a productive life. No duty is more urgent than that of returning thanks. People who aren't thankful for what they've got aren't likely to be thankful for what they're going to get. Ingratitude never finishes.

"Attitudes sour in the life that is closed to thankfulness. Soon selfish attitudes take over, closing life to better things" (C. Neil Strait). The person who forgets the language of gratitude will never find herself on speaking terms with happiness.

Thanksgiving, you will find, creates power in your life because it opens the generators of your heart to respond gratefully, to receive joyfully, and to react creatively.

> There are three enemies of personal peace: regret over yesterday's mistakes, anxiety over tomorrow's problems, and ingratitude for today's blessing.
>
> William Ward

Know you are blessed. If you can't be satisfied with what you've reached . . . at least be thankful for what you've escaped. I remember several years ago driving to dinner, completely absorbed in thought about my latest book. I was so focused, in fact, that I drove right through a red light at a major intersection in the city where I live. After being greeted by several horns and one man who wanted to let me know with his finger that I was "number one," I pulled into a parking lot and gave thanks to God for His protection . . . even when I'm stupid.

We all have a lot to be thankful for. We all have a lot to be thankful for!

Thank God and count your blessings at every opportunity. The words *think* and *thank* come from the same Latin root. If we take time to think more we will undoubtedly thank more. When you start to find fault with all you see, it is time to start looking for what's wrong with you.

I like what Dwight L. Moody said: "Be humble or you'll stumble." There's a connection between pride and ingratitude. Henry Ward Beecher pointed out, "A proud man is seldom a grateful man, for he never thinks he gets as much as he deserves." Don't be a person who has a highly developed instinct for being unhappy. Instead, "Be glad for all God is planning for you. Be patient in trouble, and prayerful always" (Rom. 12:12 TLB). The best rule is to gratefully receive whatever God gives. If we spend our time thanking God for the good things, there won't be any time left to complain about the bad.

Take some time today and sincerely consider how many things you have to be thankful for. Consider writing them down and keeping that list easily available to you. As you do, I guarantee creative ideas will spring forth from the discussion you are having with yourself. One of the most creative ways to generate momentum and opportunities is to sit down and write a note, place a call, or send an email to say thank you to those people who have influenced your life. Try to do this for as many people as you genuinely can.

There's nothing worse the earth produces than an ungrateful person. Our real prosperity lies in being thankful. Appreciative words are the most powerful force for good on the earth. Kind words don't cost much, but yet they accomplish much.

Count God's blessings, don't discount them. Pray this prayer: "God, you've given so much to me. Give me one more thing—a grateful heart."

NUGGET
#37

You Can Never
Trust God Too Much

Many people believe in God, but not many *believe God*. One of the most incredible places we can live our lives is in a continual position of believing God. "God made us, and God is able to empower us to do whatever He calls us to do. Denying we can accomplish God's work is not humility; it is the worst kind of pride" (Warren Wiersbe).

The person who puts God first will find God with him right up to the last. "In everything you do, put God first, and he will direct you and crown your efforts with success" (Prov. 3:6 TLB). Unless it includes trusting God, it's not worthy of being called His direction. Every divine direction we receive from God includes Him.

"God never made a promise that was too good to be true" (D. L. Moody). One of the great things about believing God is found in Luke 18:27, where Jesus says, "The things which are impossible with men are possible with God." When you join together with Him in His plan, things that were impossible now become possible. The superior person seeks success in God. The small person seeks success in self. You've never tapped God's resources until you have attempted the impossible.

You may trust the Lord too little, but you can never trust Him too much. With His strength behind you, His love with you, and His arms underneath you, you are more than sufficient for the days ahead of you.

> I trust that God is on our side. But, it is more important to know that we are on God's side.
>
> Abraham Lincoln

The fact is, anyone who doesn't believe in miracles is not a realist. Look around—nothing is more real than miracles. When you leave God out, you'll find yourself without any *invisible* means of support. Nothing great has been achieved except by those who dared believe God inside them was superior to any circumstance.

To say "impossible" always puts you on the losing side. If you dream big, believe big, and pray big, do you know what happens? Big things! Most of the things worth doing in history were declared impossible before they were done. What's possible is our highest responsibility.

If you put a buzzard in a pen six or eight feet square and entirely open at the top, the bird, in spite of his ability to fly, will be an absolute prisoner. The reason is that a buzzard always begins a flight from the ground with a run of ten or twelve feet. Without space to run, as is his habit, he will not even attempt to fly but will remain a prisoner for life in a small jail with no top.

If dropped into an open tumbler, a bumblebee will be there until it dies unless it is taken out. It never sees the means of escape at the top but persists in trying to find some way out through the sides near the bottom. It will seek a way where none exists until it completely destroys itself.

Don't be like the buzzard and the bee, struggling with problems and frustrations, not realizing your answer is right there above you.

The way each day will look to you all starts with *whom* you're looking to. Look to God. Believe God. When you believe God you will see an opportunity in every problem, not problems in the middle of every opportunity. Proverbs 16:3 is true when it says, "Commit to the LORD whatever you do, and he will establish your plans" (NIV). Joshua 1:9 also says, "Yes, be bold and strong! Banish fear and doubt! For remember, the Lord your God is with you wherever you go" (TLB).

All great things have God involved in them. Dare to go with God farther than you can see right now. If something is beneficial for you, God will put it within your reach. One psalm in the Bible says, "No good thing will he withhold from them that walk uprightly" (Ps. 84:11). Never undertake anything for which you wouldn't have the conviction to ask the blessing of heaven. A small person stands on others. A great person stands with God.

NUGGET #38

Live Truly and You Will Truly Live

You can't make wrong work. Never chase a lie. Left alone, it will run itself to death. Everything you add to the truth you inevitably subtract from it. It's discouraging to think how people nowadays are more shocked by honesty than by deceit. But truth is essential to society. Thomas Jefferson said, "Honesty is the first chapter of the book of wisdom."

"Those that think it is permissible to tell 'white lies' soon grow color-blind" (Awson O'Malley). We punish ourselves with every lie and reward ourselves with every right action. A lie adds to your troubles, subtracts from your energy, multiplies your difficulties, and divides your effectiveness.

"Truth is always strong, no matter how weak it looks, and falsehood is always weak, no matter how strong it looks" (Phillips Brooks). Never view anything as an advantage to you that will make you break your word. In the war between falsehood and truth, falsehood wins the first battle, truth the war. "If we live truly, we shall truly live" (Ralph Waldo Emerson).

The truth needs no crutches. If it limps, it's a lie. A lie stands on one leg and a truth on two. Proverbs 11:3 says, "A good man is guided by his honesty; the evil man is destroyed by his dishonesty" (TLB).

> Truth is such a valuable possession that you have to guard over it carefully, and you'll find that life is an uphill battle for the person who's not on the level.
>
> Joan Welsh

Liars are never free. The Bible says, "You will know the truth and the truth will set you free" (John 8:32). I'm sure the reverse is true. If you lie, a lie will make you bound. "The darkest hour of any man's life is when he sits down to plan how to get money without earning it" (Horace Greely). Instead, "refuse the evil, and choose the good" (Isa. 7:15). "Dishonest gain will never last, so why take the risk" (Prov. 21:6 TLB). The fact is, ill-gotten gain is always scattered by the devil.

When you stretch the truth, others can see through it. When you stretch the truth, watch out for the snap back. Make your word your bond. Broken promises are the world's greatest accidents. Honesty always lasts longest; a lie never lives to be old.

Truth exists. Only lies are invented. Truth shines in the darkness. "There is never an instant's truce between virtue and vice. Goodness is the only investment that never fails" (Henry David Thoreau).

"It makes all the difference in the world whether we put truth in the first place or in the second place" (John Morley). As scarce as the truth is, the supply has always been in excess of the demand. Wrong is wrong no matter who does it or says it. Truth doesn't cease to exist because it's ignored, and it doesn't change because it's not believed by a majority of people. It's always the strongest argument.

NUGGET
#39

We're All in This Together—
By Ourselves

Every great idea and dream must be established between you and God alone. There will come times where only you and He will believe it is going to happen. Can you stand alone? There's power in the principle of standing alone and being alone.

"The cynic says, 'One man can't do anything.' I say, 'Only one man can do anything'" (John Gardner). Nobody can do it for you . . . no one will do it for you. "Not in the clamor of the crowded streets, not in the shouts or plaudits of the throng, but in ourselves are triumph and defeat" (Henry Wadsworth Longfellow). You can't delegate your thinking, dreaming, or believing to others.

Thomas Edison, who claimed he could think better because of his partial deafness, said, "The best thinking has been done in solitude. The worst has been done in turmoil." Even God declares, "Be still, and know that I am God" (Ps. 46:10).

Eagles fly alone, crows fly in groups. Know how to get away. Don't belong so completely to others you don't belong to yourself. The fact is, we're all in this together—by ourselves.

> Don't keep forever on the public road. Leave the beaten path occasionally and drive into the woods. You'll be certain to find something that you've never seen before. One discovery will lead to another, and before you know it, you will have something worth thinking about to occupy your mind.
>
> Alexander Graham Bell

All really big discoveries are the result of personal thought and prayer. A reasonable amount of time alone is indispensable, but it should primarily be time spent preparing to return to the battle. Be sure to spend some time alone on a regular basis. Make appointments with yourself!

Don't accept that others know you better than yourself. Great leaders have always encountered violent opposition from mediocre minds. The biggest mistake you can make is to believe you work for someone else. You work for yourself and God's plan for your life.

The power to succeed or fail is yours, and no one can take that away unless you let them. Learn to be alone and stand alone, or nothing worthwhile will find you.

NUGGET
#40

Be Easily Satisfied with the Very Best

Start every task thinking how to do it better than it's ever been done before. "Start a crusade in your life to dare to be your very best" (William Danforth). Become a yardstick of quality. Do the right thing regardless of what others think. Most people aren't used to an environment where excellence is expected.

"It is a funny thing about life; if you refuse to accept anything but the best, you very often get it" (Somerset Maugham). Think only of the best, work only for the best, and expect only the best. Excellence is never an accident. "There is a way to do it better . . . find it" (Thomas Edison). There's always an excellent way of doing everything. "Hold yourself responsible for a higher standard than anybody else expects of you. Never excuse yourself" (Henry Ward Beecher).

> It is those who have this imperative demand for the best in their natures and those who will accept nothing short of it, that hold the banners of progress, that set the standards, the ideals for others.
>
> Orison Marden

> Happy is the man who doesn't give in and do wrong when he is tempted, for afterwards he will get as his reward the crown of life that God has promised those who love him. (James 1:12 TLB)

Excellence measures a person by the height of one's ideals, the breadth of one's compassion, the depth of one's convictions, and the length of one's persistence. People will always determine your character by observing what you stand for, fall for, or lie for.

Perfection, fortunately, is not the best alternative to mediocrity. A more sensible alternative is excellence. Striving for excellence rather than perfection is stimulating and rewarding; striving for absolute perfection—in practically anything—is frustrating and futile. We are what we repeatedly do. Excellence, then, is not an act but a habit.

"I advise you to obey only the Holy Spirit's instructions. He will tell you where to go and what to do, and then you won't always be doing the wrong things your evil nature wants you to do" (Gal. 5:16 TLB). Human excellence means nothing unless it works with the consent of God. "Excellence demands that you be better than yourself" (Ted Engstrom).

There's always a heavy demand for fresh mediocrity—don't give in to it. Instead, be easily satisfied with the very best. When you're delivering your very best, that's when you'll feel most successful.

Your character is your destiny. Never sell your principles for popularity or you'll find yourself bankrupt in the worst way. Dare to be true to the best you know.

NUGGET #41

Measure Your Life by Its Donation, Not Duration

You can succeed best and quickest by helping others succeed. "Nobody cares how much you know until they know how much you care" (John Cassis). Life is a lot like the game of tennis: those who don't serve well end up losing. We make a living by what we get; we make a life by what we give.

A man once asked renowned author and psychiatrist Dr. Carl Menninger, "What would you advise a person to do if he felt a nervous breakdown coming on?" Most people expected him to reply, "Consult a psychiatrist." To their astonishment he replied, "Lock up your house, go across the railroad tracks, find someone in need, and do something to help that person."

"Never tire of loyalty and kindness. Hold these virtues tightly. Write them deep within your heart" (Prov. 3:3 TLB). "Unless life is lived for others, it is not worthwhile" (Mother Teresa). "A self-centered life is totally empty, while an empty life allows room for God" (Tom Haggai). If you're dissatisfied with your lot in life, build a service station on it. A good way to forget your troubles is to help others out of theirs.

Serving others is never entirely unselfish, because the giver never fails to receive. "Your own soul is nourished when you are kind; it is destroyed when you are cruel" (Prov. 11:17 TLB).

> At the close of life the question will not be "How much have you got?" but "How much have you given?" Not "How much have you won?" but "How much have you done?" Not "How much have you saved?" but "How much have you sacrificed?" It will be "How much have you loved and served?" not "How much were you honored?"
>
> Nathan Schaeffer

"Selfishness is the greatest curse of the human race" (W. E. Gladstone). Self-interest is a fire that consumes others and then self. Since nine-tenths of unhappiness is selfishness, think instead in terms of what the other person wants.

> The measure of life is not in its duration, but in its donation. Everyone can be great because everyone can serve.
>
> Peter Marshall

When you're serving others, life is no longer meaningless. "One thing I know; the only ones among you who will really be happy are those who have sought and found how to serve" (Albert Schweitzer). You can't help another without helping yourself. "The liberal soul shall be made fat: and he that watereth shall be watered also himself" (Prov. 11:25).

A genuine servant seeks the success of others. The true purpose of a leader is to help others get from where they are to where they haven't been. We increase whatever we praise, and the deepest need in human nature is the need to be appreciated and praised. "Few things in the world are more powerful than a positive push. A smile. A word of optimism and hope. A 'you can do it' when things are tough" (Richard DeVos). Look for ways to help others by praising them.

No one achieves greatness without being of service. Never reach out your hand unless you're willing to extend an arm. The roots of happiness grow deepest in the soil of service. Happiness is like potato salad—when shared with others, it's a picnic. From now on, any definition of a successful life must include serving others.

NUGGET #42

Do Today What You Want to Postpone Until Tomorrow

The devil's favorite strategy to get you to fail is procrastination. Realize now is the best time to be alive and productive. If you want to make an easy job seem difficult, just keep putting off doing it. "We're all fugitives, and the things we didn't do yesterday are the bloodhounds" (*Prism*). "A duty dodged is like a debt unpaid; it is only deferred and we must come back and settle the account at last" (Joseph Newton). Work is the best thing ever invented for killing time.

What holds us back? "There are those of us who are always about to live. We're waiting until things change, until there is more time, until we are less tired, until we get a promotion, until we settle down—until, until, until. It always seems there is some major event that must occur in our lives before we begin living" (George Sheehan). *One* of these days is really *none* of these days. The by and by never comes. The person who desires but doesn't act breeds stagnation. And you should always expect poison from standing water.

About the only thing that comes to those who wait is old age. You can't build your reputation on what you're going to do tomorrow. Do today what you want to postpone until tomorrow. "Do not allow idleness to deceive you; for while you give him today, he steals tomorrow from you" (H. Crowquill). Nothing is so fatiguing as the eternal hanging-on of an uncompleted task. When you run in place, everyone will pass you by.

When people get into a habit of wasting time, they are sure to waste a great deal that doesn't belong to them. "One day, today, is worth two tomorrows" (Ben Franklin). What may be done at anytime . . . will be done at no time. "Life is like a taxi, the meter keeps a-ticking whether you're getting somewhere or standing still" (Lou Erickson). The successful person is someone who went ahead and did the things others never got around to.

A mother repeatedly called upstairs for her son to get up, get dressed, and get ready for school. It was a familiar routine, especially at exam time.

"I feel sick," said the voice from the bedroom.

"You are not sick. Get up and get ready," called the mother, walking up the stairs and hovering outside the bedroom door.

"I hate school and I'm not going," said the voice from the bedroom. "I'm always getting talked about behind my back, making mistakes, and getting told off. Nobody likes me, and I've got no friends. And we have too many tests. It's all just pointless, and I'm not going to school ever again."

"I'm sorry, but you are going to school," said the mother through the door, continuing encouragingly. "Really, mistakes are how we learn and develop. And please try not to take criticism so personally. And I can't believe that nobody likes you—you have lots of friends at school. And yes, all those tests can be daunting, but we are all tested in many ways throughout our lives, so all of this experience at school is useful for life in general. Besides, you have to go—you are the principal."

What the fool does in the end, the wise man does in the beginning. Prolonged idleness paralyzes initiative. "Don't stand shivering upon the banks; plunge in at once and have it over with" (Sam Slick). Tomorrow is the busiest day of the week. If there's a hill to climb, don't think waiting will make it any smaller.

A sluggard takes a hundred steps because he wouldn't take one in due time. If possible, make the decision now, even if the action is in the future. A reviewed decision is usually better than one reached at the last moment. "The fool with all his other thoughts, has this also; he is always getting ready to live" (Epicurus). He who fiddles around seldom gets to lead the orchestra. There is danger in delay. It's always better to reap two days too soon than one day too late. Pity the man who waits until the last day.

> "Tomorrow I will live," the fool does say; tomorrow itself
> is too late; the wise live yesterday.
>
> Martial

While the fool is enjoying the little he has, I will hunt for more. The way to hunt for more is to utilize your odd moments. . . . The man who is always killing time is really killing his own chances in life.

Arthur Brisbane

NUGGET
#43

Give God the Same Place in Your Heart That He Has in the Universe

A frequent prayer I pray for myself is found in Psalm 51:10, which says, "Create in me a clean heart, O God; and renew a right spirit within me." I've discovered this prayer has been a key to momentum in my own life. There's a supernatural confidence, expectancy, and peace that comes when we have a clean heart and a right spirit before the Father.

Once upon a time an atheist wanted to create a case against the upcoming Easter and Passover holy days. He hired an attorney to bring a discrimination case against Christians and Jews because of these observances. The argument said that it was unfair that atheists had no such recognized days.

The case was brought before a judge. After listening to the passionate presentation by the lawyer, the judge banged his gavel and declared, "Case dismissed!"

The lawyer immediately stood and objected to the ruling, saying, "Your honor, how can you possibly dismiss this case? The Christians have Christmas, Easter, and other holy days. The Jews have Passover, Yom Kippur, and Hanukkah. Yet my client and all other atheists have no such holidays."

The judge leaned forward in his chair and said, "But you do. Your client, Counsel, is woefully ignorant."

The lawyer said, "Your honor, we are unaware of any special observance or holiday for atheists."

The judge said, "The calendar says April 1 is April Fools' Day. Psalm 14:1 states, 'The fool says in his heart, there is no God.' Thus, it is the opinion of this court that if your client says there is no God, then he is a fool. Therefore, April 1 is his day. Court is adjourned."

It's just dumb not to believe in God. You can see God everywhere, if you just look. Keep your heart right. "The righteous shall move onward and forward; those with pure hearts shall become stronger and stronger" (Job 17:9 TLB). A pure heart brings increased strength to your life. Keep your heart right, especially when it's sorely wounded. You're known by the way you talk, walk, and balk.

Do what's right. If you don't want the fruits of sin, then stay out of the devil's orchard. You can't be caught in a place you don't visit. Evil that goes unchecked grows. Evil that is tolerated poisons you and all those you care about.

Just be honest with yourself. That in itself opens many doors for God to move in your heart and spirit. Say to yourself what you would be, then do what you have to do. Admit where evil might lead you, and then do what you have to do to stay free. Keep your heart pure and be blessed. Jesus says in Matthew 5:8, "Blessed are the pure in heart." The psalmist also says, "Be strong and let your heart take courage, all you who hope in the LORD" (Ps. 31:24 NASB).

Keep true and never be ashamed of doing right. Decide on what you think is right and stick to it. Hope, faith, and a right spirit will literally starve despair. Despair is not handled by giving in. It is handled best by giving out. It's nice to be important, but it's always more important to be nice.

No power in the world can keep a first-class person down or a third-class person up. There's always a high cost to low living. Give God the place of supremacy in your heart that He holds in the universe. Allow Him to create a clean spirit and a right heart in you. Let *Him* lift you up.

NUGGET #44

The Worst Liars in the World Are Your Own Fears

It's never safe to look into the future with eyes of fear. "Worry is the traitor in our camp that dampens our powder and weakens our aim" (William Jorden).

> Worry is faith in the negative, trust in the unpleasant, assurance of disaster, and belief in defeat. . . . Worry is a magnet that attracts negative conditions. Faith is a more powerful force that creates positive circumstances. . . . Worry is wasting today's time to clutter up tomorrow's opportunities with yesterday's troubles.
>
> William A. Ward

Let him have all your worries and cares, for he is always thinking about you and watching everything that concerns you. (1 Peter 5:7 TLB)

Never make a decision based on fear, and never fear to make a decision. Worry comes when human beings interfere with God's plan for their lives. Don't ever find yourself giving the "benefit of the doubt"—doubt has no benefit.

What causes most battles to be lost is the unfounded fear of the enemy's strength. Never look at your uncertain future with eyes of fear. A. Parnell Bailey says worry is like a fog:

The Bureau of Standards in Washington tells us a dense fog covering seven city blocks, one hundred feet deep, is composed of something less than one glass of water. That amount of water is divided into some 60,000,000 tiny drops. Not much there! Yet when these minute particles settle down over the city or countryside, they can blot out practically all vision. A cup full of worry does just about the same thing. We forget to trust God. The tiny drops of fretfulness close around our thoughts and we are submerged without vision.

Scott Williams shares this story:

Ron Wayne was one of the original Co-founders of Apple. Ron Wayne along with Steve Jobs "Jobs" and Steve Wozniak "Woz" were the original Apple Founding Trifecta. Wayne is actually responsible for designing the company's original logo. The Apple Logo has evolved into what we have come to know as the forbidden fruit that looks like Adam or Eve took a bite out of. Wayne also wrote the original Apple manual and drew up this start-up company's partnership agreement.

Wayne set himself up for financial success and the original agreement gave him a 10 percent ownership stake in Apple, a position that would be worth $22 billion dollars today if Wayne had held onto it. Instead of holding onto it, Wayne dropped it like it was hot. Ooops, Bad Move!

According to Mercury News, Wayne was afraid that Jobs' wild spending and Woz's life of bling before bling was bling would cause Apple to flop. Wayne decided to step down from his role of being the "mature one" in the bunch. Wayne took a bite out of the Apple and left the company after only 11 days. Wayne was a little more worried than Jobs or Woz because he was the only one of the three founders with assets that creditors could seize; he sold back his shares for $800. Let me repeat that last line . . . Wayne sold his shares for $800.

One of the best discoveries you can make is to find you *can* do what you were afraid you couldn't do. Fear and self-sabotage lock people's minds against fresh ideas. When you are ruled by fear, you'll find yourself unable to make the very changes that will eliminate it.

An old man was asked what had robbed him of joy in his life. His reply was, "Things that never happened." Do you remember the things you were worrying about a year ago? How did they work out? Didn't you waste a lot of fruitless energy on account of most of them? Didn't most of them turn out to be all right after all?

Dale Carnegie

"God never built a Christian strong enough to carry today's duties and tomorrow's anxieties piled on top of them"

(Theodore Ledyard Cuyler). The psalmist found the best way to combat fear: "But when I am afraid, I will put my confidence in you. Yes, I will trust the promises of God. And since I am trusting him, what can mere man do to me?" (Ps. 56:3–4 TLB).

NUGGET #45

If God Is Your Father, Please Call Home

Prayer brings momentum. It lifts the heart above the challenges of life and gives it a view of God's resources of victory and hope. Prayer provides power, poise, peace, and purpose for a person's purpose, plans, and pursuits. The most powerful energy anyone can generate is prayer energy. "The devil smiles when we make plans. He laughs when we get too busy. But he trembles when we pray" (Corrie ten Boom).

> Don't worry about anything; instead, pray about everything; tell God your needs, and don't forget to thank him for his answers. If you do this, you will experience God's

peace, which is far more wonderful than the human mind can understand. (Phil. 4:6–7 TLB)

God is never more than a prayer away from you. When you feel swept off your feet, get back to your knees. "If I could hear Christ praying for me in the next room, I would not fear a million enemies. Yet distance makes no difference. He is praying for me" (Robert Murray McCheyne). Heaven is ready to receive all those who pray.

Too many Christians don't pray; they only beg. Don't beg; *talk* to God. "Time spent in communion with God is never lost" (Gorden Lindsay). Martin Luther would say, "I have so much to do today that I shall spend the first three hours in prayer." When we pray, we link ourselves with God's inexhaustible power.

"Wishing will never be a substitute for prayer" (Ed Cole). Remember, prayers can't be answered until they are prayed. "What things soever ye desire, when ye pray, believe that ye receive them, and ye shall have them" (Mark 11:24). "A day hemmed in prayer is less likely to unravel" (Anonymous).

When we pray, we must simultaneously be willing to take the action God requires as answers to our prayer. "Prayer is not monologue but dialogue; God's voice in response to mine is its most essential part" (Andrew Murray). The prayers a person lives on her feet are no less important than those she says on her knees. "Practical prayer is hardest on the soles of your shoes than on the knees of your trousers" (Osten O'Malley).

The highest purpose of faith or prayer is not to change your circumstances but to change you. Pray to do the will of God in every situation; nothing else is worth praying for. "Do not have your concert and tune your instruments afterwards. Begin the day with God" (James Hudson Taylor). Prayer may not change all things for you, but it sure changes you for all things. Prayer is the stop that keeps you going. If God is your Father, please call home.

NUGGET

#46

Let Go So You Can Lay Hold

You're not free until you've been made captive by God's supreme plan for your life. Only those who are bound to Christ are truly free. In His will is our peace.

Something significant happens when we become wholly yielded to Him. "For the eyes of the Lord search back and forth across the whole earth, looking for people whose hearts are perfect toward him, so that he can show his great power in helping them" (2 Chron. 16:9 TLB).

"If a man stands with his right foot on a hot stove and his left foot in a freezer, some statisticians would assert on the average, he is comfortable" (*Oral Hygiene*). Nothing could be farther from the truth. God doesn't want us to live our lives with one foot in heaven and one foot in the world. He wants all of us.

A woman parked her brand-new Lexus in front of her office, ready to show it off to her colleagues. As she got out, a truck passed too close and completely tore off the door on the driver's side. The woman immediately grabbed her cell phone, dialed 911, and within minutes a policeman pulled up. Before the officer had a chance to ask any questions, the woman started screaming hysterically. Her Lexus, which she had just picked up the day before, was now completely ruined and would never be the same, no matter what the body shop did to it.

When the woman finally wound down from her ranting and raving, the officer shook his head in disgust and disbelief. "I can't believe how materialistic you are," he said. "You are so focused on your possessions that you don't notice anything else."

"How can you say such a thing?" asked the woman.

The cop replied, "Don't you know that your left arm is missing from the elbow down? It must have been torn off when the truck hit you."

"Oh no!" screamed the woman. "Where's my tennis bracelet?"

It's pretty clear—let's take our minds off ourselves. D. L. Moody said, "It does not take long to tell where a man's treasure is. In fifteen minutes of conversation with most men, you can tell whether their treasures are on earth or in heaven." As a young man, Billy Graham prayed, "God, let me do something—anything for you." Look at the worldwide fruit of that simple but heartfelt prayer.

When you see God's hand in everything, you can leave everything in God's hands. You must *let go* so you can *lay hold*. When you have nothing left but God, then for the first time you become aware God is enough. As soon as you cannot keep anything from God, you show your love for Him. "The most important thought I ever had was that of my individual responsibility to God" (Daniel Webster).

The world has rarely seen what God can do with, for, and through a person who is completely yielded to Him. What and how you worship determines what you become. Anything that changes your values will change your behavior for better or for worse. Corrie ten Boom advised, "Don't bother to give God instructions. Just report for duty."

Martin Luther sums up being fully yielded this way: "God created the world out of nothing, and as long as we are nothing, He can make something out of us."

NUGGET
#47

Don't Postpone Joy

Enthusiasm makes everything different. You can't control the length of your life, but you can control its width and depth by adding fun and enthusiasm. When you have enthusiasm for life, life has enthusiasm for you. "He that is of a merry heart hath a continual feast" (Prov. 15:15). William Ward said, "Enthusiasm and persistence can make an average person superior; indifference and lethargy can make a superior person average."

"Always be joyful. Always keep on praying. No matter what happens, always be thankful, for this is God's will for you who belong to Christ Jesus" (1 Thess. 5:16–18 TLB). Don't postpone joy. Joy is the most infallible sign of the presence of God. It's the echo of God's life within us. Enthusiasm is an inside job.

A little girl walked to and from school each day. Though the weather one morning was questionable and clouds were forming, she made her daily trek to school. As the afternoon progressed, the winds whipped up, along with lightning. The mother of the little girl felt concerned that her daughter would be frightened as she walked home from school. She also feared the electrical storm might harm her child.

Full of concern, the mother got into her car and quickly drove along the route to her child's school. As she did, she saw her little girl walking along. At each flash of lightning, the child would stop, look up, and smile. More lighting followed quickly, and with each flash, the little girl would look at the streak of light and smile.

When the mother drew up beside the child, she lowered the window and called, "What are you doing?"

The child answered, "I am trying to look pretty because God keeps taking my picture."

Face the storms that come your way with a smile of hope.

Enthusiasm and pessimism are contagious. How much of each do you spread? You can succeed at almost anything for which you have unlimited enthusiasm. "It's difficult to remain neutral or indifferent in the presence of a positive thinker" (Denis Waitley).

One of the single most powerful things you can do to have influence over others is to smile at them. You're never fully dressed until you wear a smile. The best face-lift is a smile. A smile is an asset; a frown is a liability. Some people grin and bear it; others smile and change it. "Be like the Mona Lisa. She keeps smiling when her back's to the wall" (Shelby Friedman).

"In my experience, the best creative work is never done when one is unhappy" (Albert Einstein). Every success of genius must be the result of enthusiasm. For every opportunity you miss because you're too enthusiastic, you will miss a hundred because you're not enthusiastic enough. I prefer the foolishness of enthusiasm to the indifference of logic.

If you find yourself dog-tired at night, it may be because you growled all day. Learn to laugh at yourself. A person with a great sense of humor may bore others, but he never has had a dull moment himself. "Of all the things God created, I am often most grateful He created laughter" (Chuck Swindoll). Humor is to life what shock absorbers are to automobiles.

You will rarely succeed at anything unless you have fun doing it.

NUGGET
#48

Build on Victories

Simply stated, there are two predictable times when a person is most likely to quit: after a mistake or after a victory. How many people of great potential have you known? Where did they all go? Most people of great potential stop because they don't build on their victories.

Success has made failures of many people. So don't quit after a victory—*build*! If at first you do succeed ... try something harder.

Once you're moving you can keep moving. Each victory only buys an admission ticket to a more challenging opportunity. The greatest benefit of a success is the opportunity to do more. "Opportunities multiply as they are seized" (John Wicker). The more you do—the more you *can* do.

Perhaps it is a good thing that you haven't seen all your dreams come true. For when you get all you wish for, you will be miserable. To be forever reaching out, to remain unsatisfied is a key to momentum.

North Carolina Christian Advocate

People who are satisfied with what they have done will never become famous for what they will do. Thomas Edison said, "Show me a thoroughly satisfied man and I will show you a failure."

The first step toward getting somewhere is to decide you're not going to stay where you are. When you have a victory, comfort and money will come, but don't confuse comfort with happiness and money with success. It's not what you get that makes you successful; it's what you're continuing to do with what you've got.

> Remember this your lifetime through—
> Tomorrow, there will be more to do.
> And failure waits for all those who stay
> With some success made yesterday.

John Wooden

NUGGET
#**49**

Love Opens

What force is more potent than love?

Igor Stravinsky

Love is the most important ingredient of success. Without it your life will echo with emptiness. Jesus said, "By this shall all men know that ye are my disciples, if ye have love one to another" (John 13:35). There is a simple way to live a life of love: breath in God's Spirit, and you'll exhale His love.

We're all born for love. It's easy to hate and difficult to love. Love will find a way; everything else will find an excuse. "Let love be your greatest aim" (1 Cor. 14:1 TLB).

A man went to a barbershop to have his hair cut and his beard trimmed as always. He started to have a good conversation with the barber who attended him. They talked about so many things and various subjects. Suddenly, they touched on the subject of God.

The barber said, "Look, man, I don't believe that God exists as you say so."

"Why do you say that?" asked the client.

"Well, it's so easy, you just have to go out in the street to realize that God does not exist. Tell me, if God exists, would there be so many sick people? Would there be abandoned children? If God exists, there would be neither suffering nor pain. I can't think of a God who permits all of these things."

The client stopped for a moment in thought, but he didn't respond so as to prevent an argument. The barber finished his job and the client went out of the shop. Just after he left the barbershop, he saw a man in the street with long hair and a scraggly beard. It seemed to have been a long time since he had his hair cut, and he looked so untidy.

Then the client again entered the barbershop and said to the barber, "Know what? Barbers do not exist."

"How come they don't exist?" asked the barber. "Well, I am here and I am a barber."

"No!" the client exclaimed. "They don't exist, because if they did there would be no people with long hair and beards like that man who walks in the street."

"Ah, barbers do exist. What happens is that people do not come to us."

"Exactly!" affirmed the client. "That's the point. God does exist; what happens is people don't go to Him, look for Him, and actively look for ways to help others. That's why there's so much pain and suffering in the world."

Love people more than they deserve. Never lose a chance of saying a kind word to another person. "You will find as you look back upon your life that the moments when you have really lived, are the moments when you have done things in a spirit of love" (Henry Drummond).

"Constant kindness can accomplish much. As the sun makes ice melt, kindness causes misunderstanding, mistrust, and hostility to evaporate" (Albert Schweitzer). Kindness has converted more sinners than zeal, eloquence, or learning. Practice constant kindness.

Augustine described love: "What does love look like? It has hands to help others. It has the feet to hasten to the poor and needy. It has the eyes to see misery and want. It has the ears to hear the sighs and sorrow of men."

> For a moment, love can transform the world. Love is life
> . . . and if you miss love, you miss life.
>
> Leo Buscaglia

To be loved, be loveable. Make it a point to love someone who doesn't deserve it, and "most important of all, continue to show deep love for each other, for love makes up for many of your faults" (1 Peter 4:8 TLB).

The Bible says, "We know that we have passed from death unto life, because we love the brethren" (1 John 3:14). Do all things with love because love opens, love asks, love expands, and love creates.

NUGGET #50

Never Let Yesterday Use Up Too Much of Today

Yesterday ended last night. So today it's more valuable to look ahead and prepare than to look back and regret. Don't let regrets replace your dreams. "A man is not old until regrets take the place of dreams" (John Barrymore). Regret looks back. Worry looks around. Faith looks up.

Life can be understood backward, but it must be lived forward. The past should be viewed with gratitude for the good things God has done, so look backward with gratitude and forward with confidence.

Your past is the start of your fresh start. Consider what Vivian Laramore said: "I've shut the door on yesterday and thrown the key away—tomorrow holds no fears for me, since I've found today." Use the past as a launching pad, not a lawn chair. Dreams of the future are more valuable than the history of the past. "The wise man looks ahead. The fool attempts to fool himself and won't face facts" (Prov. 14:8 TLB).

Experience is at best yesterday's answer to today's problem. It should only be a guide, not a jailer. Your past is not your potential. Never build your future around your past. The past is over. You must be willing to shed part of your previous life. If past history were all that mattered, librarians would be the most successful people in the world.

God doesn't review your past to determine your future. "Remember ye not the former things, neither consider the things of old. Behold, I will do a new thing; now it shall spring forth; shall ye not know it? I will even make a way in the wilderness, and rivers in the desert" (Isa. 43:18–19).

"Keep your eye on the road, and use your rearview mirror only to avoid trouble" (Daniel Meacham). Stop taking journeys into the past. Don't make the mistake of letting yesterday use up too much of today.

NUGGET
#51

Alphabet for Momentum

A Agreement
B Boldness
C Creativity
D Desire
E Endurance
F Focus
G Gratitude
H Hope
I Integrity
J Jesus
K Kindness
L Loyalty
M Mercy

N Nurture
O Opportunity
P Peace
Q Questions
R Risk
S Servanthood
T Timing
U Unity
V Values
W Willingness
X e(X)traordinary
Y Yearn
Z Zeal

**NUGGET
52**

Everyone Needs a Faith-Lift

Faith can rewrite your future. "The only thing that stands between a man and what he wants from life is often merely the will to try it and the faith to believe that it is possible" (Richard DeVos). Faith is like a flashlight; no matter how dark it gets, it will help you find your way. "Every tomorrow has two handles; we can take hold by the handle of anxiety or by the handle of faith" (Henry Ward Beecher).

All great leaders have one common spiritual gift—faith. God always holds something for the person who keeps faith in Him: "he is a rewarder of them that diligently seek him" (Heb. 11:6). Your life will shrink or expand in proportion to your faith.

Think like a person of action; act like a person of faith. Prayer is asking for rain; faith is carrying the umbrella. You must first be a believer if you want to be an achiever. "Faith, in its very nature, demands action. Faith is action—never a passive attitude" (Paul Little).

Faith is not a pill you take but a muscle you use. Faith is when your hands and feet keep on working when your head and others say it can't be done. Active faith is necessary for victory.

By faith you can be decisive in the absence of certainty or in the presence of indecision. Faith is not daydreaming; it is decision making. "Real faith is not the stuff dreams are made of; rather, it is tough, practical, and altogether realistic. Faith sees the invisible but it does not see the non-existent" (A. W. Tozer). "It is like radar that pierces through the fog, the reality of things at a distance that the human eye cannot see" (Corrie ten Boom). The world says, "Seeing is believing." Faith says, "Believing is seeing."

Faith is like a toothbrush. You should have one and use it daily, but you shouldn't try to use someone else's. "All I have seen teaches me to trust the Creator for all I have not seen" (Ralph Waldo Emerson). Doubt is the great modern plague. But faith can cure it. Real faith will refuse to see anything that is contrary to the Bible. It won't look at the circumstances or conditions but at the promise.

> Doubt sees the obstacle, faith sees the way;
> Doubt sees the darkest night, faith sees the day;
> Doubt dreads to take a step, faith soars on high;
> Doubt questions, "Who believes?"
> Faith answers, "I."
>
> Anonymous

A Final Word

I wrote this book to help you capture and increase momentum in your life. With God's help you can go as high and as far as He wants you to. You can't be anything you want to be, but you can be everything God wants you to be.

Be the original person God intended you to be. Don't settle for anything less. Don't look back; look forward and decide today to take steps toward His plan for your life.

Receive His momentum for your life. Let go of anything that makes you want to stop short of His best. Know God will continue to perform His will in you.

Remember 1 Thessalonians 5:24, where it says, "Faithful is he that calleth you, who also will do it."

John Mason is an international bestselling author, minister, executive author coach, and noted speaker. He's the founder and president of Insight International and Insight Publishing Group. Both organizations are dedicated to helping people reach their dreams and fulfill their God-given destinies.

He has authored twelve books, including *An Enemy Called Average, You're Born an Original—Don't Die a Copy*, and *Know Your Limits, Then Ignore Them*, which have sold over 1.4 million copies and have been translated into thirty-five languages throughout the world. His books are widely regarded as a source of godly wisdom, scriptural motivation, and practical principles. His writings have been published twice in *Reader's Digest* along with numerous other national and international publications.

Known for his quick wit, powerful thoughts, and insightful ideas, he's a popular speaker across the US and around the world.

John and his wife, Linda, have four children: Michelle, Greg, Michael, and David. They reside in Tulsa, Oklahoma.

John welcomes the opportunity to speak at your church, conference, retreat, or business organization.

Also, if you have any prayer requests, feel free to contact his office. He can be reached at the following:

P.O. Box 54996
Tulsa, OK 74155
Phone: (918) 493-1718
Email: contact@freshword.com
www.freshword.com